Ties That Bind

Youth & Drugs in a Black Community

Kojo A. Dei

John Jay College of Criminal Justice

WAVELAND

PRESS, INC.

Prospect Heights, Illinois

In Memory of Pooh Pooh Shields (1968–1991)

For information about this book, contact:
Waveland Press, Inc.
P.O. Box 400
Prospect Heights, Illinois 60070
(847) 634-0081
www.waveland.com

Cover: Skjold Photographs

Ties That Bind

"Kids and adults all want the same thing, except we get in trouble for it."

—18-year-old Denise

Contents

Preface

The seeds for this book, which I dedicate to Ms. Pooh Pooh Shields,* were sown in the mid-1980s when I went to Belize in Central America to study the impact of emigration on agriculture. I undertook that fieldwork in order to fulfill a requirement in the Doctoral Program in Applied Anthropology. My desire at the time was to write a dissertation on migration. My main finding that the migration of young men and women from Belize to Southern California was directly related to the increase in the cultivation of cannabis in that Central American country, from where marijuana was smuggled into the United States through Mexico, led me to study drug use among Black youths in the United States. As an African born and raised on the continent of Africa, my study of drug use by Black youths has been a fascinating study of Black experience in the African Diaspora. My focus on drugs and Black youths is simply a phase in my attempt at comprehending the conditions and behavior of Africans in the Americas.

I dedicate this book to the memory of Ms. Pooh Pooh Shields, brutally murdered a day after I had spent an entire day hanging out

---

* To maintain confidentiality and anonymity to my informants, all names of persons, institutions, and major locations have been changed.

with her and talking about illegal drugs in the Southland section of Fayerville. Pooh Pooh told me that she had decided to quit using illegal drugs (especially crack) so that she could go to college and study child psychology; unfortunately her dream could not be realized. It is the hope of her mother, Mrs. Shields, that the four-year-old daughter she left behind will fulfill this dream.

I owe a debt of gratitude to many people and foundations for helping me with the research and writing of this book, but it is not possible to acknowledge them all here. I simply want to express my sincere appreciation and gratitude to the many young people and their parents and guardians as well as the other residents in the Southland section of Fayerville. Without their cooperation and tolerance of my "intrusion" into their daily lives for a very long time (1990–2001), this presentation on Black youths' involvement with illegal drugs would be only perfunctory. I must mention the names of two special colleagues: I would like to very much thank Professors Serena Nanda and Dorothy Bracey of the Department of Anthropology, John Jay College of Criminal Justice, for their unwavering support, mentoring, and assistance without which this manuscript might not have been completed or seen the light of day. Their counsel and encouragement helped me to publish my first book! Also, I would like to thank Professor Linda-Anne Rebhun of Yale University for her extensive comments on the manuscript of this book. I'm deeply gratified by the decision of Dr. Irene Glasser to write the study guide for this book on short notice. I would also like to take this opportunity to thank my wonderful colleagues at the Thematic Studies Program (TSP) at John Jay College of Criminal Justice and my many former students who directly or indirectly helped me in this research. Last but not least, I want to thank my editor at Waveland Press, Jeni Ogilvie, for her most helpful editing of my manuscript.

The arduous task of writing this book, as indicated earlier, began a little over a decade ago with the start of my dissertation research, funded by the Social Science Research Council (SSRC). Upon completion of the dissertation, I received two summer research grants from the PSC-CUNY that enabled me to continue my ethnographic study of Black youths and illegal drugs in the same Southland community. Another source of financial assistance was the National Institute on Drug Abuse (NIDA), which offered me a pre-doctoral fellowship with the former Narcotic and Drug Research Institute (NDRI) and subsequently a Minority Research Supplementary Award. These monies allowed me to work in the field as long as I did, and I'm deeply indebted to them. However, the responsibility for all that is expressed in this book rests entirely with me and in no part with these funding agencies or the many people who helped me.

Finally, I wish to express my deepest gratitude and special thanks to my wife Mariama for supporting me emotionally during the period of what appeared to be endless revisions.

CHAPTER 1

Minorities and Drugs

Involvement with illegal drugs is endemic to the entire United States and is so widespread throughout this nation that the distinguished medical historian David Musto (1973) refers to it as the "American Disease," afflicting all age groups, regardless of racial or ethnic affiliation or social class status. The National Institute on Drug Abuse (NIDA) estimates that there were approximately 15 million people in the United States who used illegal drugs on a regular basis in the early 1990s, when this study began (NIDA, 1991). Of these, over 75 percent were White, 15 percent were Black, and 8 percent were Latino. These figures have fluctuated somewhat during the last few years, but they would be even larger if one were to add individuals whose involvement with drugs does not include use—for example, young people who sell but do not smoke crack.

One of the consequences of drug use or drug dealing that the NIDA figures fail to reflect, however, is the devastating impact of drugs in predominantly minority neighborhoods. Although Blacks and Latinos do not make up a high percentage of regular drug users in the United States, their communities suffer from crimes associated with drugs far more than other communities (Harrell and Peterson 1992). For instance, survey data consistently indicate that Blacks and Latinos

1

are more at risk than any other racial or ethnic groups of becoming addicted to hard drugs such as crack and heroin (NIDA 1991). Blacks constitute less than 15 percent of the United States population, yet they account for more than 60 percent of known crack addicts and 40 percent of known heroin addicts in this country (NIDA 1991:34). In its 1998 annual report on *The State of Black America*, the national Urban League, a major civil rights organization, concluded that substance abuse was "the single major leading social, economic, and public health problem confronting the African American Community."

Mostly teenagers between the ages of 12 and 17 and young adults between the ages of 18 and 24 carry out the distribution of illegal drugs in inner-city Black neighborhoods (Ray and Ksir 1996). The tragic consequences of their involvement with illegal drugs has prompted one commentator to label young Black males living in the inner cities as "an endangered species" (Gibbs 1988). Even a cursory review of some of the repercussions of Black youth involvement with illegal drugs makes it quite clear why such opinions are expressed frequently. Since the advent of crack in 1985, drug-related homicide has become the leading cause of death among young Black males in the inner cities (Gibbs 1988). In the 1990s over 50 percent of young Black males in prisons throughout the United States were there for drug-related offenses (Lusane 1991:22–25). In Washington, D.C., this figure rose to approximately 70 percent. It was reported in the *Washington Post* (July 28, 1995) that by the end of 1994, half of all Black males between the ages of 18 and 24 were either incarcerated or placed under court supervision in 34 counties in the state of Florida, due to drug-related offenses. As if these figures were not disturbing enough, there was also great concern about the frequent unprotected sexual activity related to drug use, which is partly responsible for the spread of HIV and other sexually transmitted diseases among Black youths (Ratner 1993). Thus, a focus on illegal drugs *within* the Black community is a legitimate concern and by no means should be interpreted otherwise.

Yet despite the dangers associated with Black youths' involvement with drugs, the climate of racial polarization in this country has led to much opposition to research (and even frank discussion) of illegal drug activities within the Black community. There are two types of critics: (1) "conspiracy theorists," mostly grassroots political activists with a radical political agenda, and (2) "antidrug crusaders," consisting of mostly elected Black officials, mainstreamers committed to working within the system toward reforms. The grassroots political activists do not believe that the flood of illegal drugs into predominantly

Black neighborhoods can be halted. They argue that it is part of a conspiracy designed to keep Blacks addicted and thus remain less of a threat to White supremacy. Of course Black elected officials reject this idea and attribute widespread drug use and drug dealing by Black youths to the high unemployment among Black males.[1] So, there is a palpable racial undertone to the debate on illegal drugs in this country, which must be brought into the open and dealt with forthrightly.

PURPOSE OF THE STUDY

This text explores the integration of illegal drug activities (processing, packaging, distribution, usage, and other ancillary tasks) in the life of a community—a predominantly low-income Black neighborhood in the northeastern United States.[2] I present portraits of five young Black men and women, ranging from 16–21 years of age at the time I began my research in 1990, and analyze their involvement with illegal drugs— mostly marijuana, cocaine, crack, heroin, and angel dust. I focus on these 16 to 21-year-olds because they constitute the cohort mostly caught up in the so-called "war on drugs." I examine the sociocultural context of their daily lives with particular emphasis on major social processes such as enculturation (the ways in which young people learn to become responsible adult members of their community) and informal social sanctions affecting their using and/or selling illegal drugs.

My intent is to shed light on the dynamic processes buried in the intricacies of ordinary social interactions as well as on the links between the local community and the political economy of the United States. Thus, I describe, for example, the private and public roles of significant adults, which contribute to shaping the young people's attitudes and behaviors toward illegal drugs and alcohol. My primary purpose is to tease out the insider's knowledge and meaning of drugs in the lives of Black teenagers and young adults for whom involvement with illegal drugs remains a persistent and widespread phenomenon. I do not presume that the marginalization of Black youth in U.S. society is principally due to their involvement with drugs. Rather, Black youths' involvement with illegal drugs may reflect the extent of their alienation from mainstream U.S. society (cf. Nobles 1984:243–250).

Often news media reports of Black youths involved with illegal drugs depict them as out-of-control criminals—junkies, crackheads, dopefiends, or potheads—a homogenous collection of individuals who prey on their own people. In contrast to such images, the portraits of the five young Black men and women presented in this book indicate that there are significant differences among young people who are involved with illegal drugs. Even though they live and operate in the same inner-city neighborhood, there are remarkable differences in the patterns of their drug involvement as well as the subsequent consequences. What these portraits reveal is that whether or not a young person becomes a drug user or peddles any of the drugs previously mentioned depends to a large extent on the *attitude*s of his or her immediate adult relatives (significant adults) toward illegal drugs and alcohol. I do not imply that only young people whose uncles or aunts or older sibling use or abuse drugs eventually become involved with drugs. Instead, the five case studies presented here demonstrate that the reaction of significant adults to a young person's involvement with drugs depends on such external factors as the character of the relations between the community and the police, the young person's role in his or her household, publicly expressed opinions about him or her by neighbors, and the young person's status among his or her peers. Thus, while focused on particular individuals, this study also reveals community attitudes and collective perceptions regarding illegal drugs, which interact with but are different from attitudes and perceptions in the larger U.S. society.

Against this background, I make the following three major points: First, contrary to the thinking of many social commentators, policymakers, and local newspaper editorial writers, drug use or drug dealing per se is not considered a major problem by residents of the community I studied. The perception and norms surrounding the use and sale of illegal drugs in this community thus differ significantly from those of the dominant U.S. culture. Second, while channels of cultural transmission such as schools, media, and peer groups are important in this community, as they are in all complex urban societies, adult household and family members as well as neighbors constitute the essential bedrock of cultural transmission. Significant adults act as "cultural mentors" to the younger members of the community, and the household in particular provides a rich locus of social or cultural learning about illegal drugs and alcohol. The attitude of significant adults may not necessarily cause young people in this or any other community to experiment with illegal drugs, but it has a profound influence. Third, a cultural perspective, based on direct, long-term, and intensive observation (ethnography), is essential in gaining authentic knowledge of a community, particularly when illegal activities are involved. This cultural knowledge can provide useful data for formulating an effective national drug policy.

THE SETTING

The setting for this ethnographic study is Southland, a predominantly Black (90+ percent) and low-income neighborhood in Fayerville (a pseudonym), a suburb of Metropolitan Central City in Marlborough County, located in the northeastern United States. The city of Fayerville covers a small area—4.24 square miles, but has a population of over 70,000 residents, making it one of the most densely populated cities in the United States.[3] Southland, which consists of roughly seven census tracts, had 28,734 residents according to the preliminary results of the 2000 census.

Overcrowding and congestion influence the pattern of drug use and distribution in Southland. For example, crack houses and shooting galleries, which normally crop up in abandoned buildings, are nonexistent because the city administration has a policy of tearing down or boarding up abandoned buildings to prevent squatters. As a result, most adults take drugs in their own dwellings where it is difficult to conceal their drug use from their children or young dependents. In addition, the lack of privacy in the domestic sphere leads to stress, which is sometimes given as the reason for using illegal drugs. A visitor to Southland may not see much drug peddling on the streets these days because the police have successfully forced drug use and sale off the streets and behind closed doors. This development has contributed to turning the home into the central locale for drug activities (processing, packaging, distribution, usage, and other ancillary tasks).[4]

Southland shows signs of urban decay, but it is not a ghetto or a slum. It seems to suffer from perpetual poverty (in 1998 the median income was less than $18,000 for a family of four), high unemployment, poor housing and living conditions, widespread and persistent drug use and abuse, plus high rates of alcoholism as well as other indices usually associated with such areas. Remarkably, Southland is not a particularly high-crime area, even though county residents in general think it is. In the mid-1980s the local newspapers dubbed this neighborhood as "the gateway" to drugs in the county, frustrating city ad-

ministrators who work hard to project the image of Fayerville as a
desirable place for middle-class families.

Race and Social Class

Blacks have lived in Fayerville since its incorporation as a city at the
end of the nineteenth century, when their numbers were very small.
Although the World War II exodus of African Americans from the rural agricultural South to the urban industrial North reached Fayerville, it did not increase the numbers of Black residents by much until
the mid-1960s and 1970s. As is generally the pattern in the United
States, when Blacks moved to Southland of Fayerville in substantial
numbers, Whites moved out to communities in the northern part of
the county. Thus today, over 90 percent of Southland residents are
Black, 7 percent are Hispanic, and only about 1 percent of the remaining are White. Citywide, Blacks constitute about 56 percent of the
population, Whites 35 percent, and Hispanics and others 9 percent.
African Americans and Jamaicans dominate the Black community of
Fayerville, and most of them live in Southland where Fayerville's largest low-income public housing is located. This housing complex is
commonly known as the "projects," and school children tease their
peers for living in the "jets," which has a derogatory connotation.

To the casual observer, Fayerville appears to consist of only two
communities delineated by race—Southland, which is overwhelmingly
Black, and the Northside, which is largely White. A closer examination, however, reveals a more complex situation. Fayerville is actually
composed of four distinct communities organized along lines of social
class—Southland, the Westend, the Northside, and the Northeast.
However, the lower-classes are segregated on the basis of race so that
Black and White residents live in separate neighborhoods while the
middle and upper classes live in the integrated sections of the city.

This settlement pattern has resulted in the Northeast section of
Fayerville being occupied mostly by upper-class professionals of all
races. In the midsection one finds mostly middle-class Italians, Irish,
Germans, Portuguese, African Americans, and West Indians. A small
but economically vibrant colony of Asian merchants (mostly Indians,
Koreans, and Chinese) has begun to emerge in recent years in this section of town as well. Lower-class Blacks and Whites, on the other hand,

live in Southland and the Westend, respectively. Few Latinos, mostly Dominicans and Puerto Ricans, reside in Fayerville. They are interspersed in the Westend and Southland, while immigrants from Brazil, Mexico, and the rest of Central America trickle into the working-class Italian and Portuguese communities in the Westend. Fayerville's political and civic leaders like to boast that this city consists of over 90 nationalities that live together in harmony. In a sense this is true, but apart from public spaces, little social interaction takes place among the various racial or ethnic groups in this city: residents rarely socialize across racial or ethnic lines outside of places of work or in schools.

Old-timers who regularly gather in Chuck's Barber Shop, on Wayward Street, tell me that "years ago" a Black person could not buy a home in the Northside, even if he or she had the money. Now, although Blacks can live anywhere they choose, the cost of housing prohibits them from moving out of Southland. In the summer of 1999, in the upper-class section of town, a single-family home cost on average about $400,000, while in the middle-class section, the cost of a single-family home averaged about $250,000. In the lower-class sections (i.e., Southland and the Westend), a single-family house cost about $180,000. Rents follow a similar pattern.

Even though Southland is overwhelmingly Black, there are significant ethnic differences within the Black community. African Americans and Jamaican immigrants constitute the two largest ethnic groups within the Black population of Fayerville, and their young people dominate the drug scene there and in the adjacent McCarthy Hill section of the major northeastern metropolis. On the surface, the relationship between these two ethnic groups appears good. However, tension lies just below the surface. The main source of tension between African-American and Afro-Jamaican youth is competition for dominance in the drug trade as well as competition for the same kinds of low-wage employment in the health care and other service industries. Thus, limited economic opportunities in the local area (legal, or regular economy, and the underground economy) is the main source of tensions in the Black community.

Female Domestic Workers

In the 1960s, African-American and Jamaican women spearheaded Black migration from "Down South" and the Caribbean to Marlborough County, where their labor was in demand as domestic workers in the homes of affluent White families. These hardworking mothers came mostly from Virginia, Georgia, Louisiana, North and South

Carolina, and the island of Jamaica. As live-in maids and babysitters, they could not bring their own children to live with them. They could be with their own children when they weren't working, but that meant they had to purchase homes or rent apartments in a neighborhood they could afford, close in proximity to their places of work. For most of these women that meant the Southland of Fayerville. As these Black women came to live in Fayerville, White families were anxious to sell and relocate further north, so they sold their houses in the poor section of Fayerville—Southland.

There was, however, another problem these Black female migrants faced: who would take care of their children while they were at work? What most of them did was instead of sending their children to the only day-care center in the neighborhood, they brought adult relatives into their homes to take care of their children while they were at work. In some instances, this was the only option because the Black female domestic worker could only return home on her days off. This arrangement established a pattern of Black children growing up in Southland under the supervision of significant adults who were relatives or neighbors rather than their biological parents, an important issue for the context of my studies. In this manner, the history of massive Black emigrants from the South and from the Caribbean led to the establishment of Black "colonies" in suburbs surrounding major metropolitan cities throughout the Northeast. Black migration to Fayerville still continues, although current domestic workers now live in their own homes in Southland with their families and commute to jobs in private residences, nursing homes, or hospitals throughout Marlborough and neighboring counties.

Black women who work in the homes of affluent White families function as a social conduit between the two races, bringing firsthand information about the lifestyles of White people to their children and other household members. However, most of the Black residents who live in Southland have little direct contact with White middle-class lifestyles, except for what they see in films and on television or read in newspapers and magazines. It is ironic that interracial contact among the post–civil rights generation occurs much less frequently than it did before the passage of the civil rights laws in the 1960s. The younger generations of Blacks, in particular, have few direct contacts with White people living in adjacent communities. Although schools in Fayerville are not segregated by law, Blacks and Whites attend separate schools and lead separate social lives. For example, nearly 90 percent of the 2,500 students of Fayerville High School are Black, while most of their White counterparts attend private schools. Thus, even at the beginning of the twenty-first century there is *de facto* segregation in this city that helps perpetuate interracial stereotypes.

The Inner City

Most Fayerville residents generally refer to Southland as an inner-city neighborhood—that is, a community with severe and endemic economic and social problems as well as deteriorating public health conditions. Some Southland residents say that they would move out if they could afford it; they point to unwholesome conditions—bad housing, filthy streets, boarded-up stores—that prevail in their neighborhood as their source of distress. Despite this, Southland is not a slum in the classic sense of the term, although it has some characteristics usually associated with such communities. The physical condition of many buildings is basically satisfactory, the majority being multi-family homes. The city administration has a policy of tearing down buildings that become vacant if the owner does not quickly rehabilitate them. This policy is aimed at preventing squatters (mostly drug users) from occupying abandoned buildings and turning them into crack houses or shooting galleries, and it is also meant to ensure that fewer buildings become too dilapidated for occupancy.

New buildings are being built at a very slow rate, so vacant lots are found in the downtown area and there exists so much overcrowding and congestion in the homes and so much litter, broken glass, and trash on the streets that one is still aware of a basic level of poverty. Recently, Southland received a facelift, yet a semblance of urban decay—empty lots turned into garbage dumps, abandoned stores with broken windows, buildings scrawled with graffiti, and littered streets crowded with people—is still visible. Every mayor in the past two decades has formed a task force to study the problem and rehabilitate the commercial center of Southland—the Wayward Street corridor. Nonetheless a visitor to this community gets the impression of a neighborhood that has been undergoing deterioration for a very long time.

In spite of the surface deterioration and sensational reports of violent and drug-related crime by the media, since the mid-1990s, FBI crime statistics indicate that the city of Fayerville is not really a high-crime area.[5] On December 11, 1999, *The Evening Report* reported a dramatic decrease of 21 percent in serious crimes in the city of Fayerville. The same report indicated only a slight increase in drug arrests (489 in 1998 and 499 in 1999); most of the other crimes involved theft, along with aggravated assault. However, the overwhelming majority of

those arrested were Southland residents. Thus, in Marlborough
County, there is a widespread perception that Southland is a dangerous place, a high-crime area. This frustrates the local administration's
efforts to maintain Fayerville's image as a desirable location for middle-class families. (Fayerville used to be called a city of homes, but this
is no longer the case).

Although violence is not always associated with illegal drugs,
older residents in particular are quick to blame outsiders from adjacent communities for homicides, shootings, and stabbings associated
with illegal drugs, especially crack. However, police reports and arrest
records indicate otherwise. They consistently show that only a small
number of persons arrested for drug-related offenses in Southland do
not reside there. The spontaneous public outcries from the residents
give the casual observer the inaccurate impression that residents are
against illegal drug activities—which is not the case. It is more accurate to say that Southland residents tolerate illegal drug activities;
lately, even the intolerance toward crackheads that existed during the
crack epidemic in the mid-1980s has begun to ebb.

Many Black residents in the Northside of Fayerville previously re-
sided in Southland and regard lower-class Southland as the base of the
Black community of Fayerville. While participation in the social life of
Southland by Northside Black residents has declined somewhat, many
still remain active with family members still residing in Southland and
in Black organizations whose headquarters are located in Southland.
On Sundays, for example, churchgoers from the Northside and adjacent communities attend church services in Southland, after which
they will visit relatives and friends and, more often than not, patronize
a favorite ethnic restaurant in the "old neighborhood." The "deser-
tion" of Southland by the Black middle class has, however, not resulted in this neighborhood deteriorating into an underclass slum or
ghetto, as has been reported in cases from around the country, particularly in the inner-city neighborhoods of Chicago (Wilson 1987).

Unlike their working parents, Black youths residing in the Northside go to the Southland every day, because, they say, the streets are
lively and full of people and, most important, the police tend to keep
their distance. "Playing in the streets in this area [the Northside] is a
hassle, man," said a 17-year-old Black youth who was born and raised in
Southland but later moved to the Northside with his parents. Although
he had friends in both the Northside and Southland, he preferred to
hang out in the old neighborhood. While it is true that Fayerville is socially segregated along racial lines, occasionally Black and White youths

socialize together in the Northside, although only a handful of Whites will accompany their Black friends to Southland. When Black students "cut" classes, or play hooky, they often hang out in Southland. Many say that they do not like the Northside because the adults there complain too much about the noise they make and threaten to call the police if they play ball in the alleyways or in the streets.

AFRICAN AMERICANS VS. JAMAICAN IMMIGRANTS

An important factor in the social dynamics of Southland is the rivalry between African Americans and Jamaican immigrants. Members of these two ethnic groups dominate the affairs of the Black community in Fayerville. It is no accident that the first Black mayor of this city was a Jamaican immigrant and his successor, the current mayor, is an African American. Although Fayerville has Black residents who originate from the Caribbean as well as from the continent of Africa, African Americans and Jamaican immigrants are the leading members of peoples of African ancestry in the Black community.

I use the term *Black community* here primarily as a political rather than a cultural or economic concept. It connotes a certain kind of social identity that all persons of African ancestry share in the United States. Jamaican immigrants and African Americans have similar social experiences in the United States, even though they possess distinct cultures. They may have different economic aspirations, but they share the same experience in the United States because of racism. Nigerian anthropologist John Ogbu (1991) has pointed out that there is a significant distinction between voluntary immigrants (Jamaicans) and involuntary minorities (African Americans) in the field of education, specifically academic performance. Also, for example, home ownership does not have the same meaning for African Americans as it has for Jamaicans and other Black immigrant populations. Jamaican immigrants purchase homes primarily to live in, while African Americans tend to view homeownership as a financial investment.

Another important difference between African Americans and Jamaican immigrants is found in their roles as domestic workers in the homes of White families. Among the younger generation of Black women, working in the homes of Whites as maids has lost its appeal, except among immigrant women from the Caribbean and Africa who hope to secure sponsorship for permanent residency in the United States. Nowadays, many Black women prefer to work in hospitals and nursing homes as nurse's aides or as cashiers and sales girls in retail stores. Those with some college education go on to become nurses, secretaries, computer operators, and civil service clerks.[6] Others work for the Metropolitan Central City Transit Authority, for the telephone company, and for major corporations in Central City.

Nowhere is the rivalry between these two ethnic groups more evident than among students in Fayerville High School. The sources of tension here, which lie below the surface, vary. The Jamaican students have separate social circles, just as most of their parents do in the larger community. In the school cafeteria, for example, they congregate in one corner to eat and socialize with other West Indians. Their explanation is that they are uncomfortable sitting with their African-American peers who often make fun of their accent and aggressively try to intimidate them. There is a West Indian Club at the high school that organizes cultural and social events for all students. African-American and Jamaican students are not always separate, however. Some students do show a willingness to cross ethnic lines, although these are mostly offspring of ethnically mixed parentage or the so-called Jamericans.

The term "Jamericans" refers to American-born Jamaicans both of whose parents are immigrants from the island of Jamaica. Their identity as Jamaicans living in the United States leads to their assuming the role of culture broker between the two ethnic groups and skillfully manipulating both groups to their own advantage. Their ambiguous social identity sometimes leaves them vulnerable, but in situations of extreme tension, they practice conflict resolution, impressing on the antagonists that they should unite to fight racism and not one another. Racism functions as a force that unites Blacks of different ethnicity or nationality in their common struggle against bigotry. Jamaicans who would not usually join forces with African Americans will do so at times in order to fight racism.

ECONOMICS AND THE DRUG TRADE

In the 1980s an open drug market flourished in Southland in the South Wayward Street corridor. It attracted customers or clientele from northern Marlborough County and nearby states. This led the news media to dub Southland of Fayerville as the "gateway" to illegal drugs in Marlborough County. It also led to the establishment of a police precinct in the middle of the Wayward Street corridor. The increased law enforcement actions, coupled with long-term imprisonment for those convicted of drug-related offenses, forced the open drug market to disappear in the middle of the 1990s. However, the disappearance of the open drug market did not bring an end to drug dealing in Southland, rather drug transactions were moved inside, behind closed doors.

In the 1980s, the influx of a new wave of migrants, largely young people from the Caribbean, brought in large numbers of fresh young people determined to make money to realize their "American dream." In addition, the children of the 1960s—"internal migrants" from metropolitan Central City—had reached adolescence or young adulthood in the 1980s, the stage in life when young people are most likely to become involved with illegal drugs. Furthermore, the Reagan-Bush administration in the 1980s marked a time when the inner cities, filled with ethnic and racial minorities, were abandoned by the government and left to fend for themselves. That decade saw unemployment among Black youth skyrocket to levels indicative of the depression (Williams and Kornblum 1985). During the Reagan-Bush era, Black youths in the inner cities everywhere, including Southland, turned to hustling in the underground economy: in most cases, that meant selling drugs in order to earn a living. Not all young people who turned to selling drugs on the streets did so because of the lack of alternative employment opportunities, however. Instead, it was because they preferred the "more flexible work environment free of racism and condescension by Whites," a 32-year-old African-American activist told me.

When Blacks moved to Fayerville in the 1960s and 1970s in large numbers, the national economy was on the threshold of a recession, and Fayerville's economy was supported by revenues from small- to medium-sized industries that had moved there from Central City, as part of the industrial exodus from metropolitan centers to the suburbs. A number of factories were set up in the so-called industrial section of Fayerville, namely, Southland. Although the City of Fayerville had given tax abatements to attract these businesses, few hired any of its large population of unemployed Black residents. The economic recession of the 1980s resulted in most of these factories being closed down, sharply reducing the city's revenue base and causing a chain reaction that resulted in the loss of local businesses, including bank branches like Chase that were located in the industrial section. Food vendors, who had catered to the needs of the factory workers, were also thrown out of work.

For decades the largest employer in Fayerville was the United States Postal Service, which received high marks for its equal opportunity employment practices. But in 1997 it, too, relocated to Green Meadows, adding to the woes of local merchants, small businesses, and the local economy as a whole. Some postal workers lost their jobs because they could not easily commute or relocate to Green Meadows (public transportation is available during the day, but not for night or late-evening shifts). Other employers receiving similar praise from the Southland community for their equal employment practices include the board of education and the city and county governments. However, the prevailing economic ideology to streamline costs, as well as the size of government, have forced these traditional sources of equal opportunity employment to hire relatively fewer employees. This has meant constriction of employment for everybody but especially for Blacks.

Some residents have prospered by working for or establishing their own local businesses. The food industry dominates the local businesses in Fayerville: either in the form of retailing imported foodstuff, fruits, and vegetables from the tropics as well as produce from Florida and California, or preparing cooked meals in restaurants and small eateries that crowd this geographically small area. Merchants and retailers are mostly immigrants from China, Korea, and India who sell all sorts of cheap consumer goods in the stores on South Fourth Avenue, the main commercial street. The Asian merchants hire undocumented aliens from Central America and Mexico and pay them less than the minimum wage, creating a backlash by the Black majority who are the customers and consumers. In the early 1990s, tensions between Korean produce grocers and their Black customers were so high that you could not walk into a store without feeling it. Black customers complained about the lack of respect shown to them by Korean grocers. Koreans, on the other hand, complained about increasing thefts by some Black customers. Fortunately, few outbreaks of hostility resulted. The tension between these two racial groups still simmers beneath the surface.

When Black residents express the desire to go into business for themselves, they often mean opening a record store, restaurant, liquor store, or hairdressing salon. Others, particularly Jamaican immigrants, like to operate livery taxis or minibuses to shuttle passengers between the adjacent McCarthy Hill section of Metropolitan Central City and Fayerville. Blacks who own or operate restaurants or small eateries face stiff competition from others, such as Italians and Chinese, who operate pizzerias and takeout restaurants. Chinese restaurants and Italian pizzerias can be found on almost every street corner in this neighborhood.

The typical Black restaurateur is a female in her late thirties or early forties who has worked in the health care industry for some time and has decided to change careers. If she chooses to open a restaurant, the tendency is for her to specialize in a regional (e.g., Southern) or national (e.g., Jamaican) cuisine. Claudette is a 38-year-old Jamaican immigrant. She came to the United States in the early 1970s, and worked for many years first as a nurse's aide. Later, after attending Marlborough Community College, she worked as a licensed practical nurse (LPN), and saved about $30,000 before deciding to open a restaurant. She chose the restaurant business because she enjoys entertaining and "people always compliment my cooking."

Claudette bought a floundering restaurant from another Jamaican. She believed that the problems of this particular restaurant were due to mismanagement and failure to serve authentic West Indian dishes. Like most small business owners in this community, Claudette did not conduct a market survey to determine the viability of another West Indian restaurant in Fayerville. She simply assumed that the circle of friends who complimented her cooking would patronize it and spread the word; she was confident her skills in the kitchen and hospitality would attract customers. She renovated the old place and renamed it The Sunshine Restaurant. Customers who ate at The Sunshine Restaurant complimented Claudette's cooking and the service, but six months after she took over, it had yet to turn a profit.

Claudette had spent almost all her savings on renovating the restaurant. Strapped for cash, she turned to her 43-year-old brother, Trevor, who lived in Fort Lauderdale, Florida. He was willing to loan her the sum she needed to cover the mounting bills, but with an important condition. He demanded that his sister allow him to sell small quantities of marijuana out of her restaurant. Claudette said she was reluctant, but unable to "see me dream go down the drain, I said yes, man." Trevor had promised her that it would be done with the utmost discretion and that only marijuana would be sold to a limited number of reliable customers. Claudette now says that Trevor deceived her and added cocaine to the menu without informing her. She made a conscious decision not to get involved with the clandestine drug retail business because "it was his [Trevor's] business." Because Trevor lives in Florida, he insisted that Claudette hire a 65-year-old Jamaican, who used to be the common-law husband of their mother, to assist her in the kitchen and handle the drug distribution.

A few months after Claudette accepted this arrangement, the restaurant began to make a profit. It slowly but steadily developed a clientele of not only West Indians but African Americans and some Whites as well. Meanwhile Trevor was arrested in Florida for gun possession, which precipitated an investigation that led the police to raid The Sunshine Restaurant. They seized large quantities of marijuana and about a kilo of cocaine. Claudette was arrested but later released, as the police investigation concluded that she did not know and did not participate in the distribution of the drugs. Following her release, Claudette sold the business to another Jamaican couple and went back to work in a nursing home as an aide. The Sunshine Restaurant survived because it had attracted a significant number of regulars who did not go there to buy marijuana or cocaine.

Claudette's experience and similar stories have tarnished the image of Jamaicans in small business, especially restaurant owners; restaurants are rumored to be fronts for drug dealers. However, the police are reluctant to target Jamaican-owned businesses that operate as fronts for drug dealers. I discussed this issue with an old timer who expressed an understanding of the police department's decision. He observed that when these businesses are shut down "new owners invariably take over because people have to work to pay their bills and taxes." He added, "Everyone understands that. . . . The cops do what they are told by the political bosses." This is an example of how the police purposefully ignore the drug dealing that goes on in this neighborhood and the young people are aware of that. Some of my teenage informants talked about such lapses in antidrug enforcement in this neighborhood as a "joke," and not to be taken seriously.

FACTORS SURROUNDING DRUG USE

Overcrowding

Among the most serious problems affecting the majority of Fayerville's residents is the lack of affordable housing. Over 80 percent of household heads interviewed mentioned lack of affordable housing as the second most worrisome problem facing their household (the number one concern being unemployment, or lack of adequate income). This has created much overcrowding and congestion, especially in Southland, where it is not uncommon to find families doubled and even tripled up in single-family houses and one- or two-bedroom apartments. In large part this overcrowding is due to the lack of new housing construction for low-income and middle-income families.

Overcrowding has resulted in illegal conversions of private homes into apartments or boardinghouses to help pay the mortgage. Most single-family and two-family homes currently have twice the number of people living in them as allowed by law. One two-family home on South First Avenue, owned by a Jamaican woman, has been converted into a three-family dwelling. The owner occupies the first floor with her family of four and rents the second floor to another Jamaican couple with little children, while the basement is rented to a single woman from St. Kitts. She took in a roommate in order to cope with the burden of $650 monthly rent.

In addition to the lack of privacy that overcrowding has created, it has also influenced the pattern of drug use and distribution. For example, there is little opportunity for adults who smoke marijuana or crack at home to conceal such activity from their children. Lack of privacy leads to stressful situations at home, which is sometimes given as the reason for resorting to the use of illegal drugs. A 36-year-old mother of two put it this way: "I'm stressed at work and wanna come home to relax, but there is no relief at home either 'cause of this [overcrowding and congestion]. Without reefer to calm me down I don't know what I'm gonna do." This woman lives in a small, one bedroom apartment with her two children, a niece, a younger brother, as well as an older brother who comes around every now and again seeking a place to stay. Like most tenants in her building, she would like to move to a bigger apartment but is unable to find an affordable one.

Welfare

It is currently difficult for single mothers to qualify for Aid for Dependent Children (AFDC) as a result of welfare reform. The Personal Responsibility and Work Opportunity Act of 1996 compels welfare recipients to seek employment, thereby effectively ending six decades of guaranteed cash assistance to single mothers with dependent children. This welfare reform legislation has hit young single mothers very hard, though even before the latest welfare legislation, the arduous process of applying for public assistance deterred some potential applicants from attempting to seek assistance (see, e.g., Valentine 1978). An applicant had to be prepared to spend long hours in the halls of the Marlborough County Social Services Department, waiting to be shown the proper way to complete and submit the forms. Then she had to be interviewed by two or three different bureaucrats before her application was subjected to a rigorous background check in order for a final decision to be made.[7] Low wages, inadequate benefits, and high rents made Southland residents perceive public assistance as an indispensable source of supplementary income, rather than as the temporary emergency assistance it was intended to be. Due to the difficulty of obtaining welfare funds, some single mothers turned to illegal drug sales to supplement their income.[8]

Family Life

Family life in Southland is greatly influenced by availability of funds and work schedules of parents. One income is rarely sufficient for young single mothers, and they may supplement their income with occasional drug sales, as you will find in the case of one of my informants—Akosua. So pulling together the incomes of all household members is necessary in order to make ends meet. Even then, the matriarch (or patriarch) of the household often must work two jobs. When this happens, the young members of the household are left at home most of the time. One way married couples try to solve this problem is by scheduling their shifts in such a way that one parent works during the day and the other works at night. While other adult members of the household may be around, they are generally reluctant to discipline other people's children on a regular basis. Because of the intense overcrowding in Southland, West Indians tend to deal with this problem by bringing in a relative to care for the younger children. The situation is slightly different in African-American households, where, increasingly, young children are sent to day-care centers when the household head is at work. Even if there is a relative at home, he or she is often reluctant to be responsible for the children. Lack of affordable housing has led to discernible changes in the composition of, as well as in relations between, members of the household (see Martin and Martin 1978). Households no longer consist only of relatives but now include strangers, such as boarders or roommates, whose rent helps homeowners to meet their mortgage payments or pay the high rents.

Lack of Recreational Opportunities

A common complaint voiced by residents of Southland concerns the lack of organized recreational activities or entertainment facilities in

Fayerville. Since the last movie theater closed in the northern side of town in the late 1980s, movie theaters, bowling alleys, and skating rinks have been extinct in the city of Fayerville, and residents have to travel to adjacent cities to enjoy such facilities. Many people argue that the lack of entertainment or sports facilities in this city adds to a social environment that is conducive to illegal drug sales. Although Southland is home to many organizations that are available for both adults and young people to join, most residents do not belong to them because of the high cost of membership fees. One of the few exceptions is the Caribbean Islands Association, which is dominated by Jamaicans whose younger members meet regularly to play dominoes and smoke marijuana. In the summer they also organize cricket matches, during which marijuana is discreetly sold. But even this group is weakened by interisland rivalries; as a result, immigrants from the smaller islands like St. Vincent, St. Lucia, or Grenada, rarely participate. Also, middle-class West Indians, who view it as a working-class association, generally also do not belong.

THE DRUG SCENE

Alcohol

Over four decades of continuous drug activities (processing, packaging, use, sales, etc.) has left indelible marks on Southland. Prior to World War II, the drug of choice of the mostly White population of Fayerville was alcohol. According to a 70-year-old retired auto mechanic whose parents moved to Fayerville from Virginia in the 1920s, bootleg alcohol created problems for young men like himself but "our sins wasn't as bad as the crack kids of today. There were fights, fists fights, and occasionally someone was stabbed but no violence as you have today. Twelve-year-olds with guns and all sorts of weapons."

Alcohol is the most popular drug of choice among all segments of the population precisely because it is not illegal and is therefore readily available. Its effects have proved particularly damaging within this community. Indeed, on numerous occasions residents suggested to me that the primary focus of my research should be on the destructive effects of alcohol. As a 44-year-old female informant observed:

> The problem in this neighborhood is not crack, it's booze. The
> cheap wine n' liquor is the real killer. Alcohol is what's destroy-
> ing the Black family not crack. As you came into the building, the
> men you saw sitting on the stoop blocking your way, they ain't
> high on crack or dope. . . . Oh, no! Don't get me wrong mister,
> they smoke reefer all right, but they are drunk and they go home
> an' take it out on our children and us [women]. We live with their
> physical and verbal abuse every day!

Most old-timers said that alcohol was the only recreational drug
they used while growing up in Southland. Even the subsequent arriv-
als of drugs like heroin, cocaine, crack, and marijuana have not dimin-
ished the popularity of alcohol, which remains very high.[9] Almost
everyone I spoke with during the course of my fieldwork admitted to
having used alcohol; this includes members of the Pentecostal
churches and the Seventh Day Adventists, who are forbidden to drink
(most admitted to having used alcohol prior to being "saved").
Among senior citizens alcohol remains the primary drug of choice.
The abuse of alcohol by senior citizens is a subject that needs to be investigated. Young people involved with drugs scoffed at the idea that
the effects of alcohol were not as devastating as that of illegal drugs.

Alcohol abuse in this community was such a serious problem
prior to World War II that Fayerville became home to a nationally
known treatment center for alcoholics. Alcoholics from the neighboring communities came to Fayerville for treatment, as they currently
do for narcotics. As other recreational substances besides alcohol
have become popular, so have drug rehabilitation programs (Open
Door, Renaissance, Archway, and a methadone clinic associated with
Fayerville Hospital).

Illegal Drugs

In the 1950s, when Whites were still the majority of the population of
Fayerville, Italians involved with organized crime controlled the narcotics distribution. They employed Black teenagers to peddle heroin,
pills, and marijuana on the blocks where Blacks lived and in adjacent
Black communities. As the numbers of Blacks increased substantially,
African Americans and Jamaicans took over the drug trade and began
to dominate the drug scene in Southland. This resulted in an increasing level of competition, as the large numbers of West Indian immigrants and Jamaican youths began to challenge their African-
American counterparts for dominance in the distribution of drugs in
this area.

Today, the drug scene in Fayerville and the adjacent neighborhood of Central City continues to be dominated by both Jamaicans and African Americans. African-American youths are involved in selling a wide variety of drugs—crack, cocaine, heroin, marijuana, and angel dust—while the Jamaican youths, on the other hand, limit their involvement to selling marijuana and cocaine powder. Interestingly, few Jamaican youths are involved with crack use and/or sale. Although these two ethnic groups do not generally compete for Black customers (each catering to its own ethnic group), they do compete fiercely for the business of White customers, who come to Southland from the northern Marlborough County to purchase drugs. This competition has led to the use of guns to kill and intimidate rivals and has become an integral part of the local drug scene. A number of residents argue that while earlier drug use was not closely associated with violence, it is the increased violence associated with crack use and distribution in recent years that has led to the increased incidence of police crackdowns.

Others, critical of city hall, complain that when organized crime controlled the drug trade in Fayerville, the police generally turned a blind eye to illegal drug activities (e.g., there were fewer police mass arrests or crackdowns). Critics charged that only after Blacks took over the drug trade did the Fayerville police begin to conduct massive arrests and crackdowns. However, in the 1970s, when Black social activists and civil rights leaders complained to the mayor that Southland residents were being used as scapegoats by the police, he ordered the police to back off to avoid accusations of racism and probable racial unrest. A longtime resident, who claimed to have been a witness to some of the meetings between Black leaders and the mayor, told me that "the police wanted to nip the drug problem in the bud [in Southland], but the White politicians wouldn't let them." He attributes this in large part to the politicians' fears of sparking a confrontation with the Black community. In addition, many Black residents in Fayerville accused the then-mayor, who was White, of playing racial politics because he needed to garner Black support to defeat his White political opponents, confirming the beliefs of some residents that "the so-called drug problem of Black youths is all politics."

Like alcohol treatment programs, drug rehabilitation programs (Open Door, Renaissance, Archway, and a methadone clinic associated with Fayerville Hospital) have become popular. These facilities, and other lesser-known programs offered by social welfare agencies and the churches in Fayerville, are all located in Southland. Despite the increased availability of treatment centers and counseling services, however, rarely do Southland residents enter these facilities voluntarily; more often they are mandated by the courts to attend such programs. Almost all of the young men and women whose portraits are presented in this book entered one or more of these facilities through court mandate. When residents do seek treatment voluntarily, it is usually for detox or overdose problems at the methadone clinic of Fayerville Hospital.

Two Perspectives: The Northside and Southland

In 1990, the Jamaican-born mayor of Fayerville set up a task force to investigate "drugs, blight and crime" in the city. The chairman of this task force confirmed that differences in perception toward illegal drugs existed between residents in Southland and those in the Northside of town. For example, Southland residents explained the widespread drug activities in their neighborhood in terms of economic necessity and complained about the lack of economic opportunities, as well as the lack of social justice. While few Southland residents actually attended the hearings of this task force—which convened on four different occasions in a local community center—those who did argued that difficult economic circumstances contribute to neighborhood residents seeking relief through the use and sale of illegal drugs and alcohol. A Black Muslim activist also correctly pointed out that selling drugs had become a substitute occupation for the large numbers of unemployed Black youths in this community.

Northside residents, however, dismissed such viewpoints and maintained that although many people in Fayerville experienced intense frustration and even despair, the majority of the residents had not turned to drugs as a solution. Privately, some of the Northside residents, including various Blacks who gave testimony, referred to Black youths who peddled drugs in Southland as "crazies," "lunatics," "parasites," and "predators" who preyed on their own community. These residents explained the drug phenomenon in terms of criminal behavior, which they perceived as being perpetrated by "out-of-control kids" under the influence of crack.[10]

At the beginning of the 1990s, middle-class Northside residents organized public protests against illegal drug activities in Southland. Interestingly enough, these protests received scant support from the predominantly working-class Southland residents, who took offense at the accusation that illegal drug activities in their neighborhood prevented middle-class families from relocating to Fayerville. The protestors demanded that the mayor take immediate action against drug peddling on the streets of Fayerville. City hall officials immediately ordered a crackdown, and scores of street-level drug peddlers were arrested. Those peddlers who managed to escape the dragnet moved their operations indoors to their own apartments or private homes. This shift led the local police to seek assistance from the federal Drug Enforcement Administration (DEA), and soon private homes and apartment buildings were being confiscated on the grounds that they functioned as "drug factories" or "supermarkets."

Thus, Fayerville became the first municipality in Marlborough County to come under the jurisdiction of the federal antidrug law, the Comprehensive Crime Control Act of 1984. However, the sweeping retribution that was directed against homeowners and apartment dwellers as a result of allegations made by a few disgruntled tenants served to turn local residents against the DEA, Fayerville police, and city hall. The mayor then quickly moved to discourage the police from confiscating local properties. In addition, the self-proclaimed antidrug crusader, Khalid Abdul, a member of a small but rapidly growing Muslim community in Southland, dismissed the protests of the middle-class residents as being orchestrated by "outsiders with their own political agenda." While he and other Southland residents voiced their disapproval of drugs, they refused to join these publicly staged antidrug demonstrations.

WHY SOUTHLAND?

Why did I choose this particular community for my reserach? Three factors influenced my decision: Perhaps the most significant factor is that I actually live in Fayerville, in an apartment less than a mile due north of Southland. Second, when I began to study illegal drugs in 1990, Southland was saturated with marijuana, cocaine, crack, heroin, and PCP, also known as angel dust on the streets. The local news media had dubbed the neighborhood the "gateway" to drugs in Marlborough County. Third, I had been associated with this neighborhood in various capacities for many years, so I assumed that access to the community would be relatively easy.

My initial contact with this community began in 1980, when the now-defunct local newspaper, *The Evening Report*, hired me. As manager of home delivery, I recruited and supervised teenagers to deliver the newspaper to private homes and offices of local businesses. Thus, I came to know not only the youngsters directly under my supervision, but also their siblings, friends, parents, guardians, and customers. Also, I became a volunteer for Operation Higher Education, Inc., a local after-school program engaged in tutoring and counseling junior high and high school students in a church basement. While my research was under way, I was appointed to be a member of the board of directors of a local nonprofit agency that provided affordable housing for low-income residents. Once again, this gave me an opportunity to know the tenants as well as other neighborhood residents who sought occupancy in buildings controlled by this agency. Southland offered me an excellent opportunity to conduct the kind of drug study that most interested me: understanding the sociocultural context of Black youths' involvement with illegal drugs.

Fayerville exemplifies the war on drugs at the national level. The middle class in the Northside is leading this so-called war, while the lower class in Southland does not see drug use and distribution as the most serious problem confronting them. Drug use is commonplace in this neighborhood. A visitor to Fayerville may not see much drug use or drug peddling on the streets, since the law enforcement apparatus has successfully forced drug users and drug peddlers off the streets and behind closed doors. This situation makes the domestic arena in Southland a particularly appropriate setting in which to explore the informal interactions between young people who are involved with drugs and their effective network of significant adults.

NOTES

[1] Not too long ago, a highly respected urban ethnographer, Elijah Anderson (1990), remarked that part of the reason the unemployment rate among young Black males was above the national average was due to the lack of old-timers willing to guide the young men as apprentices in their trades of employment. Indeed that may be the case; however, it seems that the old practice of young people learning from old folks is still functional in the underground economy, particularly with regard to involvement in the illegal drug trade (cf. Hamid 1992). Why this pattern of recruitment for the illegal drug trade persists has yet to be thoroughly investigated.

[2] I would like to stress at the outset that my focus on Black youths by no means implies that substance abuse or illegal drug activities are limited to that community only.

[3] This puts Fayerville in the top ten most densely populated cities in the United States. Fayerville's bureaucrats and social activists correctly maintain that the population is even greater. They dismiss the census figures as a tremendous undercount because most of the undocumented aliens who live in this city do not participate in the enumeration. Fayerville faced the same lack of participation by large numbers of its residents in the 2000 Census. The Planning Office estimates that the current population of Fayerville is about 70,000 and that about 10 percent of Fayerville's population may not have been counted in 2000, thus depriving the city of monies it desperately needed to provide for the increasing demand for social services.

[4] It is not uncommon to find three or more generations in a household involved in drug distribution. For example, the Hamilton household functioned as an ordinary family unit until 17-year-old Marc was arrested and his father, Courtney, hurriedly returned to his native Jamaica. Although Marc's mother, grandmother, and eight-year-old sister had assisted him in packaging the marijuana that he sold, they were not subsequently arrested.

[5] There is much controversy among criminologists about the definition of crime. Some have called for a redefinition of crime as a "violation of fundamental human rights," and not simply a violation of law enacted by the state.

[6] Southland residents prefer civil service jobs because of the good benefits and job security, which are relatively better than in the private sector. Some maintain that the real reason Blacks seek civil service jobs is that they have fewer employment opportunities in the private sector.

[7] Although employees of the social services department deny it, it is well known that the long process involved in applying for public assistance was deliberately set up to discourage illegitimate claims. Prior to the 1996 Welfare Reform Legislation, Fayerville was notorious for welfare fraud. A common scam involved welfare recipients who had regular jobs and still collected full welfare benefits as if they were unemployed.

[8] Similar to my findings in Fayerville, Jagna Sharff (1998) found that poor Puerto Rican women in the Lower East Side of New York City sold marijuana as a source of supplementary income.

[9] Since no scientific study of alcohol or illegal drugs has ever been undertaken in this community, my assessment is based solely upon my own field observations and the opinions expressed by drug and alcohol counselors in Fayerville.

[10] Of the 39 household heads I surveyed, over 90 percent considered crack to be a very dangerous drug and did not want it legalized. They put crack in a category all by itself, erroneously believing that it is instantly addictive. Many residents blamed crack for the spread of violence and increased crime in the neighborhood. Although crack was thought to be the drug of choice among young people in this inner-city neighborhood, in fact, over 50 percent of police arrests for crack possession in Southland involved adults 25 years and older. A few grandparents also were among those arrested in this neighborhood for assisting their grandchildren in packaging crack.

CHAPTER 2

Urban Ethnography

Traditionally, anthropologists have used the ethnographic method to study small-scale societies. Increasingly, however, it has been adapted to study a variety of communities in highly industrialized societies such as the United States.[1] It is the most appropriate methodology to unravel what Clifford Geertz calls the "informal logic of actual life." Ethnography involves the researcher as an empathetic participant observer in the daily activities of the subjects under study (Agar 1996). This factor, along with its holistic perspective and nonjudgmental approach, has proven especially fruitful in exploring illegal drug use and sale as a cultural phenomenon (see, e.g., Sharff 1998; Hamid 1998; Bourgois 1995).

In this chapter, I discuss some of the problems of adopting the ethnographic method to study illegal drug activities by low-income Blacks in the inner cities of the United States. My own efforts to overcome opposition by local activists to my focus on illegal drug activities within the Black community are also discussed. The discussion sheds light on an aspect of the fieldwork process that is seldom written about in ethnographies: the unpleasant and frustrating task of explaining to a skeptical group of people the value of cooperating with the ethnographer.

THEORETICAL BACKGROUND

There is a vast social science literature on illegal drug use from which three major models can be discerned: deviant behavior, drug subculture, and structural.[2] Each model addresses a different aspect of the drug phenomenon. None of them, however, adequately address the significant theme of the social or cultural meaning of drugs from the perspective of the local community. Yet it is within the local community or neighborhood that socially constructed meanings of illegal drug activities, such as processing, packaging, distribution, consumption, and other ancillary tasks, take place.

The *deviant behavior (social pathology) model* has dominated the study of illegal drug use in the United States over the past four decades (Winick 1986). This model is based on the presumption that the use or sale of illegal drugs is condemned throughout the United States as deviant or criminal behavior. Therefore, drug users and drug dealers should be treated as pariahs with amoral tendencies. These are assumptions that anthropologists in particular reject as elitist and prejudicial because they ignore the local cultural context of drug use (Partridge 1985; Dreher 1982; Rubin and Comitas 1975). In a plural society like the United States, there is no single standard of behavior, and norms and values must be viewed in light of their appropriate local setting. Furthermore, as Charles Winick (1986) correctly points out, the deviant behavior model rarely takes into account changes in patterns of drug use that have occurred since the social upheavals of the 1960s, nor does it recognize the changes in attitude toward drugs that have accompanied current trends in drug use.

The *drug subculture theory* too narrowly focuses on the use or sale of illegal drugs by individuals and their social interactions with other drug users or dealers. It presumes that drug users (and addicts) and drug dealers possess a distinctive lifestyle centered on the common bond of their drug-use behavior (Johnson 1980)—hence the claim that this group of individuals constitutes a subculture. Although this model attempts to understand the individual drug user or drug dealer, it fails to conceive of the drug phenomenon as an interactive process involving both drug users and non-drug users. As a result, the social relationship between drug users (or drug dealers) and non-drug users is arbitrarily severed without empirical justification, and the extant daily social interaction between these two categories of people is either misconstrued or not acknowledged at all. Thus the symbiotic relationship between the two groups, which Howard Becker

(1964:2) describes as being such that "one cannot exist without the other," is denied. This theory also prejudges drug-use behavior as deviant from the perspective of non-drug users (i.e., the dominant culture). Ignoring or rejecting the relationship between drug users and non-drug users has had significant consequences for such critical aspects of dealing with the drug problem, as treatment and counseling. For example, it has misled treatment and counseling providers to believe that you can provide counseling to children who use illegal drugs without the active participation of their parents or guardian (significant adults) who may not use drugs themselves.

Both the deviant behavior and drug subculture models, as indicated above, presume a split society in which people involved with illegal drugs are in constant opposition to the rest of society, that is, the larger segment of the population who are not involved with drugs. This dichotomy does not reflect empirical reality; it ignores the functional relationship of drug users and drug dealers to other important social and cultural domains in their community.

The third model, commonly known as the *structural model*, could also be referred to as the *political economy model*. This model emphasizes the significant role of economic factors while seeking to address the failure of the other two models to acknowledge the integration of drugs into U.S. culture. It does this by shifting the analytical unit of the drug phenomenon from the individual to the larger social group or community. The structural model presents a more fruitful approach than either the deviant behavior or the drug subculture model for understanding the persistent involvement with illegal drugs by Black youths. However, it has limitations that have been pointed out by critical medical anthropologists (Singer, et al. 1992). For example, it fails to pay sufficient attention to the local community or neighborhood, which is the intermediate level of analysis between the "macro" levels of cities, states, and nations and the "micro" levels of families or households and individuals. The neighborhood or local community serves a strategic function as the link between the societal and individual levels of analysis and therefore is crucial in determining the sociocultural meaning of drug-use behavior.

QUALITATIVE VS. QUANTITATIVE RESEARCH

Concern with the local community raises the question of which methodology is most appropriate for investigating the drug phenomenon.

Much of what's been written about Black youths and illegal drugs is
based primarily on surveys and quasi-ethnographic studies. The dominance of epidemiological studies aimed at mapping out the spread of
this or that particular drug epidemic is partly responsible for this. It
should also be pointed out that the study of legal substances, such as
alcohol, and illegal drugs in this country has a built-in bias in favor of
surveys because they produce quantitative data sought by policymakers who appropriate money for the National Institute on Drug Abuse
(NIDA) and similar agencies.

Qualitative data, on the other hand, are considered by some to be
less objective (i.e., unscientific), take too long to generate, and are anec-
dotal in nature. Both methodologies are legitimate; frankly speaking,
we need a reasonable balance of quantitatively- and qualitatively-ori-
ented studies of drug use. Until quite recently, the relatively few ethnographic studies that used the qualitative method were conducted
outside the United States. A combination of the two methods gives a
more comprehensive understanding and detailed knowledge of the drug
phenomenon. However, employing both methods requires greater skills
and tends to be more expensive as well as more time-consuming. My
primary interest in the sociocultural meaning of drugs led me to adopt
the qualitative method although I did conduct a limited survey of households in the neighborhood. Hence my method of study can be appropri-
ately described as the ethnographic approach and the model that guided
me is a cultural model based on Clifford Geertz's definition of culture.

THE CULTURAL-NORMALIZATION MODEL

The framework I used in this study is called the *cultural-normalization
model*. It is based on Clifford Geertz's (1973:89) definition of culture
as "an historically transmitted pattern of meanings embodied in symbols, a system of inherited conceptions expressed in symbolic forms by
which men [sic] communicate, perpetuate, and develop their knowledge about and attitudes toward life." When culture is understood in
this Geertzian sense, we are reminded that "[culture] is not a power,
something to which social events, behaviors, institutions, or processes
can be causally attributed; [rather] it is a context, something within
which they can be intelligibly . . . described" (Geertz 1973:14). With
this definition of culture, part of my aim was to consider how knowl-

edge about and attitudes toward illegal drugs were acquired and expressed in symbolic form in this community.

For Geertz, human behavior is symbolic action—action that signifies. It is through the flow of behavior that cultural forms find articulation, what Geertz (1973:17) refers to as the "informal logic of actual life." In order for an ethnographic description to bring this informal logic to light, it needs to be microscopic, focusing on the finer details of cultural expression. Therefore, using Geertz's concepts as a foundation in my examination of a neighborhood's culture, I sought to understand its residents' behavior.

The goal of a model based on the Geertzian notion of culture, then, is to expose the "normality" of a people's culture (i.e., their understandings and actions) without, at the same time, reducing their particularity. Such an approach should render a culture accessible to outside observers. At the heart of this approach is the assertion that our formulations of other people's symbolic systems need to be actor-oriented—descriptions of a culture must be cast in terms of the people's constructions of experience, the formulae they use to define what happens to and around them.

This last observation seems particularly germane to the purposes of this study, given that most attempts to analyze Black youths' involvement with illegal drugs have failed to provide an adequate consideration of the actor's point of view. Geertz alerts us to the need to grasp the subjective understandings of those individuals who choose to become involved with drugs. Furthermore, he stresses that "to look at the symbolic dimensions of social action . . . is not to turn away from the existential dilemmas of life for some empyrean realm of de-emotionalized forms; it is to plunge into the midst of them" (Geertz 1973:30).

Not everyone agrees with Geertz's notion of culture, which has been criticized for failing to recognize the contested nature of cultural meanings. This criticism is particularly relevant to a discussion of the culturally diverse Black community, or, additionally, the United States, a pluralistic, complex society in which a consensus about the meaning of many behaviors is rarely reached (e.g., consider the current debates about abortion). What the elite or even the majority of society understands as inappropriate or criminal behavior is often not regarded as such by minority segments, even though, ideologically, all groups may espouse a common belief in the legitimacy of the law. In fact, understandings of what constitutes normative behavior are seldom universal, owing to differences in ethnicity, social status, class, gender, age, and other differences (cf. Keesing 1992).

It is possible to argue that Geertz's own position points to this state of affairs. For if, as he asserts, cultures are systems of construable signs or symbols, we must allow for the fact that these symbols may be interpreted or read differently by different actors. While there may well be certain master symbols upon which everyone must agree in order to belong to the same culture, what is needed is an understanding of culture that allows for the fact that at many—if not all—levels, the meanings of these symbols are open to interpretation.

My approach is a variant of John Ogbu's (1978) cultural model used to study the poor academic performance of African-American youths in the California public school system. A cultural model, according to Ogbu, a Nigerian anthropologist, refers to a social group's own "understandings of how their society or any particular domain or institution works and their respective understandings of their place in that working order" (1991:3–33). Thus the cultural model of African Americans, for example, is based on their experience in the United States from slavery to contemporary times. Their cultural model (based on their perception of social reality) is different from that of West Indians or African immigrants living in the United States, even though politically they all belong to the so-called Black community—a point all too often ignored in most studies. Ogbu's concept of a cultural model is a major contribution in the sense that it advances our efforts to bridge the gap that exists in levels of analysis between the structural or institutional models on the one hand and the deviant behavior and drug subculture models on the other. Most important, it is the community's cultural model that proves to be more effective than the dominant cultural forms in influencing social behavior at the local level.

IN THE FIELD

Prior to undertaking my first fieldwork, I assumed that illegal drugs were the most serious social problem in Southland. Police arrests indicated this to be the case, as did local newspaper stories that reported the activities of Fayerville residents, including those from Southland, who also claimed that drug abuse was the number-one problem in their city. Thus, I made youths' involvement in illegal drugs the focus of my study of youth and adolescence. I saw the main aim of my research as understanding the paradox, or seeming conflict, between, on the one hand, the reported concerns and hostility of community residents toward illegal drugs and, on the other hand, the heavy participation of local youths in using and selling these same drugs. How was it, I asked myself, that a thriving drug trade in the streets was being carried on principally by teenagers (12–17 years old) and young adults (18–25 years old) who lived at home with their parents, grandparents, or guardians, the very people whom the newspapers reported as being totally opposed to drugs?

Later, I realized that this very question came out of my own cultural background in Africa. Coming from a village in Ghana, where obedience to one's parents and village elders is one of the most powerful cultural norms, I could not understand how young people, who were dependent on their parents or guardians, could disobey them by becoming involved in drugs. In my African village, the individual is viewed as an embodiment of the *abusua*, or family, to which he or she belongs. Our value system emphasizes the social unit of the abusua and not the individual per se. In other words, the individual member is a representative of his or her abusua and must thus find self-expression in its consensus and approval as well as that of the village community. In this sense, then, it was my outsider status as an African, with a contrasting cultural view of the proper relationships within families, that led me to focus on the family and neighbors as an important context in connection with the involvement of young people with illegal drugs.

I was confused about what these residents really felt: did they truly disapprove of drug use and drug peddling in their community as reported in the local newspaper? It was only through the ongoing process of ethnographic research that I was able to grasp an important key to understanding this apparent paradox: that for many youths involved in drugs, their network of significant adults gave only lip service to opposing drug use and sales; in reality, they conveyed a mixed message. In fact, I ultimately came to appreciate that it is the ambivalence and contradictions among adults in Southland that was the key context in which adolescents' and youths' involvement in drugs could be understood. My fieldwork revealed to me that while Southland residents publicly expressed the opinion that drugs were a serious, or even the most serious, problem in their community, they might not have meant what they said.

Many adults pointed out, for example, that nicotine, caffeine, and alcohol are worse than smoking marijuana, yet they are legal. Others frequently told me that teenagers turn to drugs because they have nothing to do; they lack jobs and there are no recreational facilities in the community. Recently, in answer to a question about the persistence of youths' involvement in illegal drugs, the mayor of Fayerville reiterated the viewpoint that drug use is mainly limited to marijuana smoking and that the lack of jobs and training opportunities are responsible for young people becoming involved in illegal drug activities.

In addition, it was only in the course of my fieldwork that I began to understand the American value of independence, which contrasts so much with my own culture. In the United States, unlike most African societies, children's individuality and independence are highly valued and American parents allow their children a great deal of freedom to find themselves and establish their own identity. Strict obedience to elders is not highly valued, and indeed, adolescence is even defined in terms of rebellion (see, e.g., Margaret Mead 1970). This helped me understand not only the behavior of young people, but also the ambivalent attitudes of many of their adult family members.

Mind Your Own Business!

As I began to focus my ethnography more on family relations and their links with the use (and sometimes sale) of illegal drugs, I had to delve more persistently into the daily and private lives of the Southland residents. My work demanded, insofar as it was possible, my active involvement in the lives of the subjects. Yet it was precisely this type of long-term personal engagement ("intrusion in the name of science," as some critics would say) that was sometimes despised, rejected, and not welcomed by many Southland residents. Their motto was "mind your own business," an attitude experienced by other researchers, including African Americans like the late Delmos Jones (1995) and other Black ethnographers. Also, savvy political activists committed to defending the rights of the working poor and those of the so-called underclass changed the dynamics of the relationship I sought to establish with informants.

The motto "mind your own business" haunted me for much of the 18 months I conducted fieldwork. Rarely did a week go by without my hearing such comments as "You [are] not in Africa; this is [America]. You shouldn't be talking like that. You ask too many questions . . . they're personal and none of your business." People who did not want to talk with me simply repeated, "Mind your own business!" Even residents who had earlier expressed their willingness to cooperate with me sometimes reneged because of what they complained was my unrelenting push for more personal information. They told me that some of my questions were unrelated to my topic, too personal, and unnecessarily intrusive. Some residents accused me of being too "pushy." Others found it incomprehensible that after spending many hours, often days, telling me their life history, I insisted on hanging around much longer. "For what?" they wanted to know. It was difficult to explain the concept of ethnography to members of the community. The following comments by a 39-year-old mother whose son sold crack were typical:

> I've told you everythin' I know [about drug use/dealing in this neighborhood]. I even talked to you about me [my life]. I don't talk like that to anybody. I've known you since you've been workin' for the paper [*The Evening Report*]. But I don't like to talk about myself like that. I did it 'cause I want to help you out with your book [dissertation]. That's why I talked to you. . . . I've told you everythin' I know. . . . Everythin'!

When asked about the details of her son's possession of crack that led to his arrest, she became irritated and obviously annoyed, raising her voice to say, "You go talk to him about that. Didn't I tell you this before?" My efforts to explain the purpose of asking her about her son's involvement with drugs provoked this sharp response: "What he does is his own business! [Do] you understand that?" Similar parental reactions were not uncommon, and they always abruptly ended our conversations, at least temporarily.

Building Trust

Like people everywhere, residents of Southland are wary of intruders or outsiders. Initially, I thought that the refusal to talk to me was due to my status as an outsider. For even though I looked like them, whenever I opened my mouth to speak it was quickly apparent that I was a foreigner, either from Haiti or Africa. A foreigner, a stranger, evokes distrust or dislike until such time that one of the "natives" concludes that he or she is "cool." Whenever my friendly overtures were rejected, I tried not to be devastated, but it left a mark on me, though it later became clear that the reluctance or even refusal of some residents to talk to me had more to do with their concern about their privacy than about me personally. An acquaintance later explained to me that African Americans were concerned about their privacy and that they were not rejecting me as an African or as a person. According to a 42-year-old schoolteacher, urban ethnographers (whom she describes as "sociologists" masquerading as anthropologists) are "very nosy people 'cause you all ask too many questions . . . that ain't none of your business." Her opinion echoed the sentiments expressed by many Southland residents.

Interestingly, I had fewer problems with the young people—the teenagers and young adults. As far as they were concerned, I was "cool" because I was a "brother from the Motherland" (Africa). From their point of view, an outsider was someone who disapproved of their drug use or drug dealing, or subscribed to the tenets of the larger U.S. society or dominant White culture. Thus, outsiders might include social workers, law enforcement officers, teachers, even other Black residents (those whom Hannerz [1969:38–42] as well as Anderson [1999] refer to as "mainstreamers"). They considered anyone who sought to impose their lifestyle on them as an outsider.

Many Southland adult residents were ambivalent about my research. On the one hand, they welcomed my quest for higher education and wanted to assist me, but on the other hand, they did not appreciate the subject of my investigation. For, as a retired elementary school teacher put it to me privately, "you don't want [to] wash your dirty linen in public in these United States," implying the racial animosity that exists in this country. The primary reason behind the criticism of this study was its focus on Black youths' involvement with illegal drugs. Some residents expressed a general concern that my study would give "ammunition" to racists and reactionary segments of our population. Others said that it would inadvertently contribute to the perpetuation of stereotypes about Blacks, stereotypes that portray us as addicts, junkies, crackheads, pimps, hustlers, prostitutes, and criminals. Community activists in particular were unrelenting in their criticism. They demanded to know who was going to benefit from the information being gathered, and they were skeptical about my suggestion that the Black community would ultimately benefit.

My graduate work in anthropology in Germany, with its emphasis on the importance of "scientific objectivity," also had not prepared me for the hostility expressed by many people in Southland. Many residents who did not understand the goals of an empirical, neutral, social-science study were not satisfied with my justification that my work would contribute in a positive way to the documentation of the social history of peoples of African descent in this country. For many of them, so-called "documentation" had not been positive. They felt that school textbooks did not accurately reflect the experience of Black people and that current textbooks were filled with negative stereotypes of Blacks. My response that the purpose of my fieldwork was to gain an insider's knowledge and skills and to acquire professional credentials to write books and articles depicting Blacks more accurately was only partially successful in answering their doubts and modifying their skepticism.

The varied concerns expressed by community members forced me to rethink the potential harm a study like this could do to some people. Of particular concern was the possibility that the police might be shadowing me and I might inadvertently lead them to a drug dealer or a fugitive from the law. Indeed, a situation like that developed when one of my informants, an immigrant from Trinidad and a Rastafarian sympathizer who operated a mom-and-pop candy store on notorious Wayward Street, was suddenly arrested after the police found large quantities of marijuana and cocaine in his store. I was disturbed by his arrest and became more alert as to who might be in my immediate environment at any point in time. I grew suspicious of persons who hung around and listened to the topic of my inquiries without saying anything. These "hangers-on" rarely contributed to any ongoing discussion. I began to restrict the types of questions I asked informants in public spaces; I waited to talk with them in private about anything that could be potentially harmful.

Prior to the arrest, I had often hung out in this candy store to observe schoolchildren who came in to buy candy or soda. The informant and his wife introduced me to a number of youthful customers who later proved to be good sources of information. Of particular concern to me was my informant's uncle, who was the real owner of the store. He did not approve of my presence in the store and was suspicious of what I did for a living. He wanted to know what was going to be done with the information I had been "collecting for months now." Unlike his nephew, he did not care about my quest for a Ph.D. and insisted that I not hide behind the scientific edict that what happens to the data is my prerogative as the researcher. It was not just my informant's uncle who demanded to know exactly who was going to see the information I was gathering and what was going to be done with it. Another "nemesis" was Khalid Abdul, a Black Muslim activist, who told me that because I was studying at a White institution, the community had to watch me and demand answers to questions such as proprietary rights to the data I was gathering.

I could not easily dismiss these concerns: although residents' demands made it more difficult for me, the persistent negative media representations and racial discrimination in this country made their concerns both understandable and valid to me. In my conversations with skeptical residents and activists I argued that, as an African, I could not remain silent or be insensitive to the negative depictions of Blacks in the media and textbooks; I was proud of my identity as an African and my identification with the struggles of African Americans. In these conversations I repeatedly stressed my determination not to allow my work to be used in ways that promoted a "savage" or "primitive" view of African-American culture, a determination that often helped reassure my African-American informants that I shared their concerns and would be sensitive to them.

In spite of all my efforts to reassure them, however, some people, mostly men, were understandably reluctant to disclose their involvement with illegal drug activities or even talk about problems in their immediate families. For example, the father of one of the five youths whose portraits appear in this book, Ron Marshall, refused to discuss the specifics of an altercation he had with his son, Gerald, despite my repeated appeals and assurances to give the incident an empathetic depiction. Ron's reluctance was perhaps due to the embarrassment he felt at that time, which was caused by Gerald's behavior. Ron was raised in the South and felt that children should not raise their voice when speaking to adults. His reluctant behavior was not unusual; I encountered other Black men who also would give me only limited cooperation. They were friendly and polite but unaccustomed to "exposing themselves," as one woman put it, or discussing details of their relationship with immediate family members with me.

Another African American I got to know well had invited me to meet his family and was instrumental in getting others to cooperate with me. However, he refused to discuss issues relating to his marital problems with me, although he disclosed his continuing use of heroin. When I asked his wife about this perplexing behavior, she said that he was reluctant to disclose this information because he resented the idea that an African could come here to attend a prestigious university, yet as an African American, a native of this country, he could only graduate from a community college. Because of the reluctance of many adult males to speak to me about family matters and about drugs, I often began conversations by asking more about such general subjects as unemployment, racism, or sports, bringing in questions about drugs and family as the conversation progressed.

As my fieldwork progressed, and the people I spoke with sensed the genuine respect I had for them and the genuine interest I had in their lives, cooperation increased. They shared with me light moments of laughter and teasing, although on a few occasions arguments resulted in mutual avoidance for several days. I was welcome in most homes, not as a researcher but as a "brother" from Africa, interested in learning about the pains and joys of growing up in an inner-city neighborhood in urban America. This acceptance was very important to me because it meant that I had succeeded in conveying to residents that I harbored no prejudice against those who used or sold illegal drugs, or who had children or close relatives who did so. I simply respected all those with whom I came into contact as human beings. Low-income Blacks, like all people, have the need to be respected in as much as the need to survive. It is perplexing that so many social scientists and commentators seldom give recognition to the need for respect and instead focus exclusively on bread-and-butter issues, as if those are the only things that worry poor people.

RECRUITMENT OF INFORMANTS

In the spring of 1990 I began to recruit young people involved with drugs and their families to participate in an 18-month ethnographic study. The purpose of the study was to explore the cultural context of illegal drug use and sale, with particular emphasis on youths' involvement. I regularly visited two alternative local high schools—the Fayerville Academy, since renamed Pan-African High School, and College Opportunities, Inc., a privately run institution that prepares students for the General Equivalency Diploma (GED). I targeted these schools because it was commonly known that their students were involved with narcotics. The Pan-African High School is a public school created by the Fayerville Board of Education specifically for junior high and high school students who otherwise would be dismissed because of disciplinary problems. Thus, its student body consisted of transfers from the regular public junior high and high schools. Most of the students at College Opportunities, Inc., on the other hand, were mandated by the courts to attend classes, either as part of their probation or in lieu of being sent to jail.

My visits to the two alternative schools involved giving a series of guest lectures on the anthropology of African societies. Following each lecture, a small group of students would gather around me to ask more questions. I turned such informal discussions into a focus group or rap session and used the opportunity to solicit information on subjects such as how I should dress when I was in their neighborhood observing and conducting my research. For example, I asked for suggestions regarding how to encourage people to talk freely about their involvement with illegal drugs and what to look for in determining whether a person is a "controlled" drug user or an addict. The students enthusiastically talked about illegal drugs and related issues, thus making my visits to the schools mutually beneficial. They were enthusiastic about the opportunity to hear from me, born and raised in Africa, which they affectionately referred to as "the Motherland," and I had the opportunity to find informants for my ethnographic study.

Two of the five intimate portraits presented in this book are based on the lives of young women who attended College Opportunities, Inc. A third case study involved a young man I assisted to enroll in this school but who later dropped out. Another informant was slated to attend the Pan-African High School but refused and dropped out of school completely. The fifth portrait is of a 19-year-old female student who attended a community college in a neighboring county. As previously mentioned, all but one of the five youths that form the core of this study were involved with illegal drugs. These five—two males and three females—and their effective networks constituted the major participants in this study. They were chosen not because of their representativeness; rather they provided illustrations of the range of youths' involvement with illegal drugs in this neighborhood. Each of them was interviewed on numerous occasions, at least half a dozen times during the initial 18 months of fieldwork. They were my key informants.

The primary techniques used to gather data were ethnographic interviews and social surveys. The informal ethnographic interviews and observations provided *qualitative* data about the five youths and their effective networks, as well as the community at large. I administered formal social surveys to collect *quantitative* data about the levels of involvement with drugs from the sample of 39 household heads and 50 youths (ranging in age from 12 to 24 years old) because no published scientific study of drug activities in this community was available. These research methods are discussed in the following sections.

ETHNOGRAPHIC INTERVIEWS

The term *ethnographic interview* refers to open-ended interviews that produce the kind of information social science calls qualitative data.

In ethnographic interviews the interviewee was, for the most part, allowed to talk freely, although I suggested the topics for discussion and controlled the general direction that the conversation took. This type of interviewing more accurately depicts what actually went on when I was engaged in participant observation. My participant observation did not involve using or selling drugs, but rather involved long talks, exchanges, discussions, debates, rap sessions, and question-and-answer sessions, as well as conversations with key informants.

The interviews covered a broad spectrum of subjects, including perceptions of drugs, the character of social relationships, informal social sanctions, employment, education, personal ambitions or aspirations, and concepts of shame and respect. The purpose of the interviews was to answer two basic questions: (1) What was the process by which young people became involved with drugs when there were legal as well as social sanctions against drugs? (2) What was the reaction of their parents, guardians, friends, and neighbors to such involvement? Additionally, the questions were intended to gain a concrete sense of what the respondents did in their daily routines and which people served as major influences in their lives.

Generally, the interviews took place in the interviewee's home. However, eventually I found it necessary to rent a storefront office in the epicenter of Fayerville's drug trade, known as the "block," so that I could more easily observe interactions between the young men and women who peddled drugs at this major intersection. This field office was also a convenient place to conduct interviews with informants who were hard to reach at home. (Many young men who peddled drugs in Southland rarely stayed at one location or address. In order to avoid arrest during raids by the police narcotics task force, they often slept in the homes of different relatives and girlfriends.) Each interview session usually lasted from one hour to three hours. Initially, I made an attempt to tape record all the interviews, but objections voiced by some participants led me to abandon this practice.

I also engaged in a form of participant observation called the *folk seminar* (Gwaltney 1993; 1981:49–52), which is a discussion group consisting of a relatively small number of people from the community under study, set up by the researcher to talk about and analyze particular themes in their lives. The researcher, in a folk seminar, acts as a group facilitator, encouraging informants to speak freely about the subject under discussion. It was convenient to adopt this form of participant observation in my study because Black men in Southland often socialized in cliques of about half a dozen members. It was hard to get the

men to agree to be interviewed one-on-one, so I quickly learned to solicit information from already-existing social units by turning these
cliques into focus groups that discussed topics of mutual interest. Similarly, I organized students enrolled in the alternative schools into focus groups or rap groups. One topic I particularly included in sessions
with these informants was how these youths perceived adults' attitudes
toward drugs in their community. Much valuable information was
gathered at these meetings with students, and they helped shape the
questions I used later on in the social surveys.

I held the folk seminars in private homes during family reunions,
in barber shops, on playgrounds, in taverns, or on the basketball
court—anywhere a small group of people gathered and were willing to
share their experiences. Many folk seminars led to understandings that
might not otherwise have been revealed. For example, during one seminar I learned that teenagers from Southland did not perceive incarceration to be a deterrent to crime. Rather, most of them thought of the
county jail as a "playground," partly due to the fact that inmates from
this neighborhood were often put in the same cell. Rarely did these
youngsters experience the isolation that detention usually engenders.

Because adult males generally were less cooperative than the
young people, I adopted the strategy of folk seminars in order to engage them in dialogue. I used this strategy, for instance, with a small
group of adult males who met regularly in Chuck's Barbershop on Wayward Street. They were retirees who had spent most of their adult lives
in Fayerville, but occasionally there were young adults among them too.
They came to Chuck's Barbershop to socialize with their peers, leaving
their wives or girlfriends at home. Sometimes these folk seminars functioned as a kind of people's court of the housing project or neighborhood, where discussions centered on issues of current import.
Occasionally I would ask a question, but mostly I would sit quietly and
listen as the men expressed their views and offered analyses of their
own and everyone else's behavior. They focused on what was wrong
with the world today. Rarely did they talk about what was good or positive in their lives because, for most, the "good times" were relegated to
the past, during the civil rights marches of the 1960s. Folk seminars allowed me to gain insight into the lives of these old-timers and how they
tried to influence the young people who looked up to them.

In order to help determine the different meanings individuals
gave to the same norm associated with drug activities, I also conducted
life-history interviews with the five youths and with some members of
their effective networks. For instance, it was clear at the outset that

differences existed between African-American and Jamaican youths
with regard to drug preferences, as well as with regard to myths associated with drugs and drug users. However, it was not clear whether significant differences existed *within* each of the two ethnic groups. The
life-history interviews were aimed at discovering such intraethnic
group differences, if indeed they existed at all. None were found.

Gender-based differences within the groups were found, and they
are reflected in the portraits of the five youths. For example, when
young mothers have to survive only on welfare payments they feel
forced to supplement their family income with income from drugs
sales, especially when their spouses or boyfriends were in prison, most
often because of drug-related offences. These same women tended to
use illegal drugs when they felt overwhelmed by their circumstances.

SOCIAL SURVEYS

As noted previously, the gap in literature on drugs in Southland
prompted me to create a database that would provide quantitative information on illegal drug activities in this community. I recruited respondents through the adoption of a technique commonly known as
snowball sampling, that is, initially I contacted a few respondents who,
after responding to my survey questions, recommended other potential respondents to me. Thus I administered two social surveys using
nonprobability sampling.[3] A brief outline of the two surveys follows.

Household Survey

The household survey was designed to provide two types of information: first, demographic data on household composition, age, income,
ethnicity, education, membership in organizations, employment, marriage or mating patterns, and religious affiliation; second, social attitudes toward, or perceptions of, the five most common illegal drugs
found in Southland (marijuana, heroin, cocaine, crack, and angel
dust) as well as alcohol and tobacco. Although the last two substances
are legal, they are notorious for endangering public health in this
community and I included them in this survey. Indeed, many local residents suggested that the focus of my study should have been on alcohol because of its devastating impact on families. Additionally, I asked

questions about drug-related problems like AIDS, as well as about other social problems primarily involving teenagers and young adults, such as dropping out of school and teen pregnancy.

I originally planned a sample of 50 households, targeting only those with teenagers or young adults. In most cases, I went door to door randomly; in other cases the households were recommended to me. However, only 39 household heads accepted the surveys, of which only 24 surveys were fully completed (the remaining 15 were partially completed). The reasons residents gave for refusing to cooperate ranged from lack of time to displeasure with questions related to drugs. Some household heads were reluctant to talk about the sources of their earnings, while others consistently underestimated their total household income.

I did not offer monetary incentives for cooperation with the household survey, but I often did small favors for respondents, such as giving them a ride to the health clinic or to shopping malls in nearby Green Meadows or Yorkville. I gave informants small gifts during Christmas and on their birthdays. Even so, it was difficult to obtain complete cooperation, and even within the two dozen completed surveys not every household member was interviewed. I had intended to interview every household member above the age of 12, since this was the typical age at which youngsters in the community began their drug careers (in the sense of using and/or selling drugs on a regular basis). But many household members were either uncooperative or rarely home, and conflicts in scheduling made it impossible to continue pursuing these individuals. Adult males (25 years and older) turned out to be the least cooperative of all the informants. They were rarely home between 10 A.M. and 10 P.M., and even when they were around, many refused to be interviewed. They did not want to talk about their own involvement with drugs and alcohol or to discuss the drug activities of their children (although a few would later talk "off the record," and in general terms, about drug use/abuse).

The most cooperative informants turned out to be females with children, mothers and grandmothers who sensed my genuine interest in their lives and readiness to assist them in small ways. As a result, I had frequent invitations to visit local churches, and I made every effort to honor as many of them as possible (I sent small donations when I could not honor the invitation).

Youth Survey

The purpose of the youth survey was to obtain quantitative data about patterns of drug involvement specifically associated with teenagers (between the ages of 12 and 17) and young adults (between the ages of 18 and 24) in order to place the five case studies in a proper generational context. Because of young people's continuing involvement with illegal drugs, the Fayerville School District had a Drug Abuse Resistance Education (D.A.R.E.) program. However, it is considered an ineffective prevention program by many in the local social services community because it is taught primarily by police officers in uniform, whom the Black community generally distrusts. The six drug treatment agencies in Fayerville at the time also offered their own prevention programs in the junior high and high schools on an ad hoc basis.

I had hoped to use the youth survey to interview 50 respondents, and it too was a convenience/purposive or nonprobability sample. The questions sought to determine the modes of drug usage as well as the frequency of use; they also probed beliefs surrounding each type of drug used, as well as expectations concerning a particular drug's psychological effects.

Unlike the adults, the young people were very cooperative. I had less difficulty getting them to answer the survey questions, and they did not hesitate to talk about their earnings, including money earned from selling drugs. (Although most of the drug peddlers I encountered were unemployed in the legal labor market, a few worked full-time or part-time at regular jobs.) Most young people who peddled drugs in Southland operated as "independents." They were seldom employees of a structured or highly organized drug ring. Organized drug rings in Fayerville had ceased to operate when I began my research in the early 1990s, as leaders of these drug rings had been arrested and were serving long prison sentences. Membership in a drug distribution network brought longer prison sentences in the state of New York because of the Rockefeller Laws mandating that stiff sentences be imposed on persons convicted for possession of even small quantities of illegal drugs.[4]

I recruited respondents for the youth survey in several ways. For instance, I compiled a list of persons arrested for drug-related offenses from the local newspaper, *The Evening Report*, which published a daily police record of arrests. Names, addresses, ages, and the specific reasons for the arrests appeared in the newspaper column "Police Watch." I recruited young people through the arrest list in *The Evening Report* and through a snowball sample, seeking out key individuals and asking them to provide a list of friends to be consulted for possible interviews.

The young people I interviewed talked about earning fantastic sums of money each week from selling crack and dope (heroin). They bragged about how crafty they were in eluding arrest. However, many later admitted to me after I got to know them better that they had been arrested and served some time in the county jail. Interestingly, many did not appear to be as concerned about having an arrest record as one might imagine. For example, when I asked one 17-year-old Black man whether he was worried about the effect his arrest might have on his future employment prospects, he responded: "Why should I be? I ain't gonna get a job from Uncle Sam. I know that . . . I don't wanna work for the government. Never! Never!" Concerning employment in the private sector, his response was immediate and just as defiant: "Forget it, [are] you kiddin'? White people don't like Black people period. I don't wanna work for no White man." This young man said he hoped either to work for himself or to look for another Black person who might give him a break.

Some youths even joked about the times they spent in jail and talked about their incarceration with what amounted to a sense of pride in doing what they wanted to do without fear of arrest by "the man" (i.e., the police). Most of these young people had spent less than a year in jail and were back on the streets.

The draconian nature of the Rockefeller Laws' mandatory long prison sentences sometimes influenced prosecutors to show leniency especially to first-time young Black arrestees. Prosecutors either changed the charge under which the suspects had been arrested or cut a deal with them that allowed the judge to sentence them to a lesser term than that prescribed by the Rockefeller Laws. Nevertheless this did not diminish the real possibility of being sentenced to prison for a very long time on the charge of possession with the intent to distribute narcotics. I asked many people about the Rockefeller Laws as a deterrent to their own involvement with illegal drugs. Apparently they were unfazed. They felt no personal or public shame in being labeled ex-convicts.[5] The law, surprisingly, does not seem to be a deterrent; as one respondent told me, "a man's gotta do what man's gotta do." Clearly, the Rockefeller Laws are an example of a failed drug policy of yesteryear, which is why *The New York Times* called for their repeal in an editorial entitled "Drug Laws That Destroy Lives" (May 5, 2000).

For the youths in Southland, life was all about getting respect among one's peers, an aspect of social life in the inner city documented in several ethnographies (see, e.g., Bourgois 1995). Yet law enforcement officials consistently fail to use such knowledge when making decisions regarding youthful offenders. For many young people growing up in Southland, "doing time" in the local or county jail

served as a rite of passage, similar in some ways to the initiation cere-
monies undertaken by African youths, where demonstrations of physical endurance and knowledge of community folklore are required.
Southland youths who spent time in the county jail exchanged stories
about con artists, drug dealers, local folk heroes, legends, and other
characters whom they had either met or heard of. If and when a young
person left jail unscathed and with reputation intact, the prisoner's
status was elevated to that of an adult. Moreover, on the basketball
court adjacent to the projects, teens and young adults could be heard
invoking cell numbers from the county jail as if these were magical
charms for good luck.

SOCIAL ATTITUDES TOWARD DRUGS

The ethnographic data I present illustrate cultural patterns and an informal logic regarding illegal drug activities. Essentially, drug use was
not frowned upon as long as it did not involve antisocial or violent behavior. Some Southland residents smoked marijuana almost as regularly as they smoked cigarettes or consumed alcohol, but they usually
did so in private. Although the use or sale of illegal drugs (except for
crack) was not generally considered to be deviant behavior in Southland, it was rarely openly spoken of as being "normal." The majority
of residents in the community did not use illegal drugs and did not
hesitate to voice publicly their disapproval of the use of such drugs. At
the same time, in private, they rarely condemned relatives, friends, or
neighbors who used and/or sold illegal drugs as long as they handled
themselves properly, that is, as long as they did not resort to violence
or other antisocial behavior. Furthermore, many people believed that
users tended, for the most part, to act in a socially correct manner
while under the influence of illegal drugs and emphasized that it was
the use of a legal drug, alcohol, that led some individuals to violate socially acceptable norms of behavior.

Young people interpreted as best they could the mixed messages
embedded in their significant adults' attitudes toward drugs. Young
people in this neighborhood, aware of the adults' tolerance, were confident that their immediate relatives, close friends, and neighbors
would not notify the police of their possession of illegal drugs as long
as they did not "mess up" or get into trouble. Some significant adults

were themselves drug users, while others disapproved of cocaine, crack, and heroin, but not marijuana.

The residents of Southland showed less concern with issues of addiction than did professionals (police, counselors) and the wider population. Southland residents had a "sociological" definition of drug addiction that differs from the mainstream medical model to which most professionals adhere. Residents believed that those who use drugs regularly and are unable to live up to their social and financial responsibilities, as a direct result of their drug use, are drug addicts. This is quite different from the medical definition: drug addiction exists when the temporary disruption of drug use leads to the onset of both physiological and psychological withdrawal symptoms (such as aches, pains, or cravings). In Southland, many persons commonly known to use drugs may not have been physically or psychologically dependent on them. These "addicts" may have used marijuana periodically, thus experiencing no physical withdrawal symptoms (Goode 1999), and they may have limited their use of cocaine and/or crack to small amounts taken only occasionally.

A young person's continued interest in drugs largely depended on the reaction of a cadre of significant adults. Southland residents commonly argued that "using drugs doesn't hurt anybody except the user," and a distinction was often drawn between drugs themselves and the crimes associated with drug use. It was hardly surprising, then, that most parents or significant adults in the Southland did not consider youths' involvement in the drug trade as a major "problem," except when it involved violence. Far from being regarded as deviant or pathological, selling drugs (particularly marijuana) was generally viewed as a positive opportunity, giving the person the chance to make a little money. Southland residents' attitudes toward drugs reflected a sophisticated understanding of the role drugs play in the underground economy of inner-city neighborhoods (cf. Hamid 1998).

Unlike law enforcement officers, who serve as "official" agents of social control in the community, significant adults functioned as "unofficial" agents of control (cf. Anderson 1980). Furthermore, their reactions to drugs were spontaneous and uncoordinated, unlike the predetermined response of police officers, drug enforcement agents, and drug counselors. These significant adults operated at home and on the streets with an informal badge of authority: the folk wisdom they had acquired, which could be used to persuade young people to adhere (or not to adhere) to the community's standards of behavior. Significant adults thus acted as instruments of social regulation in the community, expecting their proteges to do the right thing and trying to guide and, when necessary, constrain their behavior.

Because of the importance of the financial contribution the young men and women made to their households, significant adults often avoided asking about the sources of their income. In interviews with mothers whose sons were languishing in prisons for convictions of drug-related offences, many explained to me that they did not condone breaking the law (i.e., selling illegal drugs), but they insisted that their sons had to do "whatever it was they did" in order to survive. When mothers without adequate income become dependent on their teenage sons for money, as if they were their boyfriends or husbands, they develop a love-and-hate attitude toward "illegal" drugs. On the one hand, they fear that drug dealing could send their "baby" to jail or prison, yet they like the monetary benefits that come from their sons: an ambivalent attitude toward drugs in general that is prevalent among Southland residents. In this sense ambivalence simply refers to adults being simultaneously attracted to and repulsed by illegal drugs.

Another example of ambivalence is seen in the behavior of the mother of Tyrone, a friend of one of my key informants, who once told me that since she could not always trust what her 15-year-old son said, she no longer bothered to question him about his whereabouts or what he did to earn money. Tyrone, like other teenagers in this neighborhood, was well aware of this lack of supervision on the part of his mother. He interpreted his mother's reaction (or lack thereof) to mean that she did not care what he did, as long as he did not get arrested. I interpret Tyrone's mother's behavior to mean she was she was experiencing what can only be described as parental fatigue. But more important, she exhibited an ambivalent attitude toward drugs.[6]

Adult ambivalence is part and parcel of the whole cultural complex of illegal drug activities in the inner cities. It has deeper roots in social relationships, as Robert K. Merton and Elinor Barber (1963) point out in a rarely cited but significant article. Unfortunately, the drug research literature refuses to take into consideration the contradictions and ambivalence that give human affairs, including social institutions, their unique character.

Also, I realized that the two African-American youths, Gerald and Akosua, appeared to be far less concerned about adult retribution for getting caught using or selling drugs than were their Jamaican counterparts, Dread and Denise. West Indian teenagers, in general, showed a greater concern for being punished or reprimanded by their parents, or by their significant adults, if caught in possession of illegal drugs. This was probably because, in most cases, the punishment was more certain and severe than that received by their African-American counterparts. A Jamaican mother, for example, sent her 13-year-old son back home to Jamaica for insubordination after "the boy started fooling around with them cocaine."

How can the informal cultural logic of this community be explained? And what does it suggest about national response to illegal drug use in the inner cities of the United States? This study suggests that social attitudes toward illegal drugs in Black communities stem from the unique status occupied by Blacks in the United States. Low-income Blacks currently stand at the crossroads of this country's social, economic, and racial problems. They occupy a peculiar position in this society, facing a unique set of circumstances, which requires a constant struggle on their part. As a result, they tend to have a different set of priorities from those of most mainstream middle-class Americans. Ethnography can provide the key to understanding the prevalence of illegal drug activities in the Southland of Fayerville, as in other inner-city Black neighborhoods, by uncovering and illuminating the unique set of circumstances that permeates and defines the sociocultural context of life in the United States for low-income, inner-city Blacks. The findings I present in this book offer a unique perspective that complements common, popular beliefs and social science theories about drug use and distribution in the inner cities.

FIVE PORTRAITS

This study describes the lives of five young people, four of whom were involved with illegal drugs. The fifth, whom I call Liz, had numerous friends who used and sold drugs, but she managed not to use or sell drugs or become pregnant and drop out of school, as many of her friends did. Her inclusion in this study offers an opportunity to pursue questions that would otherwise have been left out. For example, Liz's family seemed to be more cohesive than the others, which facilitated discovering to what extent family dissolution is a factor in susceptibility to drug use and sale and to early pregnancy.

Two of my five key informants were males (their ages refer to how old they were at the time I did the research in 1990): Gerald was a 16-year-old African American and Dread was a 19-year-old Jamaican.

The remaining three were females whom I call Akosua (a 21-year-old African American), Denise (an 18-year-old Jamaican), and, as previously mentioned, Liz (a 19-year-old African American whose mother was from the U.S. Virgin Islands). This study draws attention to the significant role of women in the drug trade, frequently because their boyfriends or spouses have been incarcerated as a result of their involvement with drugs. Often in such situations, a young woman (often a mother) decides to sell drugs to supplement her family's meager income, as happened in the case of Akosua.

These five stories show that the initial contact with drugs most frequently occurs at home, although this does not always result in becoming a regular drug user. The term *initial contact* refers to the very beginning of the process of cognitively becoming aware of the local meaning of drugs in the immediate environment. For example, Akosua told me that when she was a preadolescent she first learned from her aunt that marijuana is an aphrodisiac. Her aunt expressed favorable feelings about sharing a marijuana joint with her boyfriend in bed. The initial contact often took place within the home and involved adult family members who openly expressed their favorable feelings about drugs. This finding both contrasts with and complements that found in the social science literature, which emphasizes that children learn about drugs primarily from peers outside the home (Carpenter, et al. 1988; Glassner and Loughlin 1987).

In Southland the home serves as the primary source of social learning about illegal drugs, whereas the streets, schools, and playgrounds—environments in which peer contacts predominate—represent a secondary initiation into the drug scene. It was at home, for example, that all the major participants in this study learned about and tried a marijuana joint, after observing an adult family member or friend light up. Only after first learning at home to identify what marijuana or cocaine looked and smelled like, as well as how to use them and identify their beneficial and potentially dangerous effects, did young people take their drug-related activities outside the home.

While young people did talk about drugs with their peers, their circle of friends also included individuals who did not want to have anything to do with drugs. Liz, for example, had friends who used and sold drugs, but she made it clear to them that she did not want them to use drugs in her presence, and they respected her wishes. At the same time, Liz expressed acceptance of the choice her friends who used and/or sold drugs had made, even though on some occasions she confided in me that they were wrong.

NOTES

[1] See, e.g., Michael Agar's *The Professional Stranger: An Informal Introduction to Ethnography* (1996).

[2] See, e.g., Erich Goode (1999) *Drugs in American Society, 5th ed.;* Ansley Hamid (1998) *Drugs in America: Sociology, Economics, and Politics;* Ed Knipe (1995) *Culture, Society, and Drugs: The Social Science Approach to Drug Use*.

[3] This sampling method is used for purposes of convenience and it avoids the more sophisticated, expensive, and time-consuming probability sampling. (For a detailed explanation of these terms or methods, see Babbie 1998.)

[4] In the current legislative session, the governor has proposed new legislation to repeal these laws because they have not deterred drug use and have instead led to tremendous increase in the prison population of this state.

[5] For a similar attitude and patterns of behavior among Black youths in Brooklyn see Donaldson 1993.

[6] Claude Brown (1965), the author of the famous book, *Manchild in the Promised Land*, encountered adult ambivalence toward heroin in Harlem in the 1960s.

CHAPTER 3

Gerald by His Own Bootstraps

The portrait of Gerald Marshall, an African-American teenager, presents a baffling image of a Black youth, demonstrating that involvement with drugs (marijuana, cocaine, crack, heroin, and angel dust) is not limited to those who come from so-called dysfunctional families or households and that members of locally recognized decent families are also involved in the use and/or sale of drugs, especially marijuana. When I met Gerald, he was an ambitious, intelligent, and funny kid who wanted to be an adult in a hurry. He thought that adulthood would earn him greater respect and the independence he so badly desired. Even though he grew up in a two-parent household, which neighbors regarded as a good home, his experiences would cause social critics to label him as a bad kid: he was a high school dropout and had run-ins with the law, but thus far had escaped being sent to jail or prison.

Sixteen-year-old Gerald Marshall had been arrested during a police drug sweep of Southland, but he was soon released. His story appeared in the local newspaper, *The Evening Report*, and as soon as I read the article, I approached his mother Brenda about talking to him.

Hoping his association with me would influence him to stay in school and perhaps go to college, she introduced me to him and persuaded him to cooperate with my research. However, the young man, who was known to be stubborn, had different ideas.

Gerald was the kind of person some members of the community called a "problem kid," yet he was loved by many who knew his family. According to the social worker who counseled Gerald and his mother, "problem kids" in this community get into trouble all the time but escape the appropriate punishment because they are considered minors by custom and juveniles by law. More troubling to Brenda was that by the age of just 16, Gerald had already been arrested for a variety of offenses, including trespassing, disorderly conduct, menacing, operating a motor vehicle without a license, and possession of a controlled substance, later identified as crack.

When Gerald was 15 a family court judge threatened to send Gerald away to a reform school for boys, located near the U.S.–Canadian border, over 300 miles from Fayerville. His mother, with support from the social services department, pleaded with the judge, saying that sending Gerald to an institution might adversely affect his parents' marriage; the judge relented. Thus, the Marshall family was spared emotional loss that would have resulted from the temporary banishment of Gerald from his hometown. However, his parents' 20-year marriage still did not remain intact, and they separated not long after the judge's decision.

GERALD AND HIS PARENTS

By local standards, Gerald, Brenda, his sister Sandra, and Sandra's little girl, Keisha, lived in a lower-middle class section of the Southland. Most of the one- and two-family, frame houses in this area were old but well maintained. Gerald's street was a well-known hangout for teenage drug peddlers, and thus the police frequently patrolled the area. The notoriety of this area rivaled that of the corridor on Wayward Street, known as "the block," which led the newspapers to dub Fayerville "the gateway" to illegal drugs in Marlborough County. In the 1980s "the block" attracted drug dealers and buyers, as well as curious onlookers from all over Southern Marlborough County and the adjacent metropolis of Central City, while Gerald's street was openly the turf of local teenagers aspiring to become "big time" drug dealers.

The house in which his family now lived was first bought and occupied by Brenda's parents until they retired to their home state of Virginia. Before his parents' separation, Gerald's father, Ron Marshall, lived with them, although he had been absent from home frequently due to his job as a long-distance truck driver. Ron has since moved to the neighboring city of Yorkville, but still visits them. Gerald has two older brothers (Ronnie and Eric Marshall) who moved away after completing high school. Ronnie, the oldest and favorite son of Ron Marshall, is in the Army and is stationed in Georgia, while Eric, the most gregarious of the Marshall children, works on the staff of a powerful congressman in Washington, D.C. As a result of the absence of these two older sons, there are unoccupied rooms in this two-family house, which are kept as guest rooms for relatives from Virginia, who visit regularly.

Gerald and his father do not get along. The older Marshall accused his youngest son of being "dumb" for becoming involved with drugs. The younger Marshall, on the other hand, accused his father of being a "hypocrite," because he took speed and smoked free-based cocaine as well as marijuana. Ron maintained that he needed the stimulants to keep him awake on the road. Gerald argued that because of his father's own drug use, "he has no right to call me names." Gerald got angry when anybody tried to put him down. He wondered why his father called him a "crackhead" for smoking crack but did not call his older brothers "potheads" for smoking pot. Was it because he (Gerald) was the youngest of the Marshall children, or that he was the only Marshall ever to be arrested for drug possession?

Gerald did not think that his arrest for drug possession warranted his father's constant ridicule, because "over here [in Southland] every kid has a record; it's no big deal." Gerald claimed he was innocent of the charge of drug possession on that particular occasion and accused the arresting officer of planting the evidence on him while he was being frisked. This is a common complaint I heard from mothers who told me about their children's arrest for drug possession. However, when the arrestee complained to the court-appointed lawyer, he or she was often told "to shut up" and plead guilty so that the outcome would be a light sentence or probation with no jail time.

The following incident exemplifies the "bad blood" between father and son. Gerald purchased a nice sports car, a Nissan 280Z, at a great discount because it needed major repairs. None of Gerald's close relatives asked him where he got the $5,700 to buy the car. When I asked his mother where her 16-year-old son got the money for this car, she said that he did odd jobs to earn money and got monetary gifts from his grandfather, which he saved to buy the car. Gerald asked his father, who had been repairing automobiles since retiring as a truck driver, to show him what to do to make this car road-worthy again. According to Gerald, instead of showing him how to fix it, Ron decided to take the car to a friend's shop in Yorkville, and there he repaired it on his own. When he returned the car about a month later, he told Gerald that he was "dumb" to buy a foreign sports car because the repairs were more costly than they were for American cars, and besides, the police would be after him all the time, as they were after all young Black men who drove fancy cars. According to Gerald, his father also told him that he did not deserve to own such an automobile because he did not understand even the simple mechanics of a car. Immediately he responded sharply to his father's criticisms, and their exchange in front of the family home got so heated that Sandra and a visiting relative had to step between them to prevent violence.

A witness to their altercation, who knew of my association with Gerald, ran to my storefront office, about three or four blocks away from the Marshall home, to inform me of the altercation. He said that he knew Gerald was one of the "kids you was studying, so I seen him and his father go at each other. I said, 'Wow! Kojo should've seen this one.' That's why I came to tell you 'cause I heard you want people [to] call you anytime somethin' like that happens."

When I arrived at the scene, I saw a small group of people, mostly neighbors, gathered on the sidewalk in front of the Marshalls' home, talking among themselves. Inside I found Sandra who said that her mother and her Aunt Trudy had gone shopping in Green Meadows and that her father had left (pointing in the direction of his favorite local bar). I found him inside Joey's Lounge, drinking beer by himself. He would not talk to me about the incident at this time, but agreed to talk about it a month later in the context of a general discussion of the behavior of young Black men. At that time he told me that he was from "Down South," where young people respected their parents and elderly people in general. We both agreed that lack of respect for one's elders implied lack of respect for one's self.

After the aborted conversation with Ron, I went back to ask Sandra about Gerald's whereabouts. As we were discussing where Gerald might be, he suddenly showed up at the door, saying that some neighbors had told him that I was looking for him. He, too, was not yet ready to discuss the incident, but he soon relented and agreed to tell his side of the story at his favorite eatery, the Yankee Cafe. I had to wait until the next day to talk to his mother when she told me about the long-standing animosity between her husband and their son.

Although Gerald was just 16 years old, he was 6' 1" tall and weighed about 180 pounds. Because of his size, strangers often believed that he was indeed 20 years old, as his fake ID declared. His neighbors expected that he would be interested in sports and that he might perhaps become a professional player in the National Football League (NFL) or the National Basketball Association (NBA). However, Gerald said that he was not interested in becoming "anybody's workhorse" who was discarded like garbage after his playing days were over. "That's slavery all over again and Black people better wake up! Wake up!" he opined, with the excitement of a teenager. Rather than athletics, Gerald's primary interest lay in becoming a musician, a recording artist, and a music producer.

His father thought that this was a "dumb" idea and accused his son of being lazy. Ron believed that Gerald had the natural ability to become a professional athlete, and thus all he needed to do was train hard to develop his God-given talent. Brenda agreed that their youngest son needed more structure and discipline in his life, which they were unable to provide at home because her work schedule (she was a counselor in a home for mentally retarded children) and because Ron no longer lived with them. However, Brenda maintained that, as parents, they should be supportive of whatever career their son was interested in pursuing.

The differences between Ron and Brenda Marshall's reactions toward their son's arrest for crack possession were sharply apparent. According to Sandra, when Gerald was arrested his father's reaction was that "if he is dumb enough to get caught, he must do the time." Ron confirmed this by saying that he did not care about what his son was going through while in police custody or the potential damage a prison experience might have on Gerald's development or future. Brenda, on the other hand, said that she was not against punishing her son if indeed he was caught with crack or any other illegal drugs. However, she expressed concern that sending a "child" to prison could scar him for the rest of his life, all for possession of something as "stupid" as crack. She resented the treatment of her son by the police, explaining, "I don't want him treated as if he's committed murder or something like that. [A Black woman] cannot abandon her son because, in this country, [the Black man] has no one else but his mom." When pressed about her son's past arrests, Brenda got a little irritated: "I don't have time to be judgmental. Do I have a choice? He needs me at a time like this more than any other time; I don't know if he's been ly-

ing to me all this time. I think the Lord gave me Gerald as a challenge
for me to become a better person." I asked her why she insisted that
Gerald remain at home when, clearly, he would not obey her orders.
She responded: "When you love somebody you can't turn him away.
He's my baby, my last one. He's gone through a lot. He is a fighter else
he won't be here today [alluding to her difficult pregnancy with him].
He didn't ask me to bring him into this world, into these United States
. . . if you know what I mean."

Brenda worried a great deal about Gerald, whom she affectionately called her "baby." She worried that he might not live to celebrate
his twenty-first birthday, as was true of many teenagers in this neighborhood. Whenever Gerald stepped outside the house, she would tell
him to be careful, but his quick response was always: "Oh mom, don't
worry, I can take care of myself. Besides, when my time is up, there is
nothin' you or anyone can do about it." Brenda would respond angrily, "Don't say that. Stop that nonsense! Just be careful, okay?" Gerald was not the kind of person who gave in easily, and he liked to tease
his mother. He reminded Brenda that about a year ago, when her girlfriend, Marble, was mourning her son who had been gunned down,
she had made similar fatalistic comments to console her friend.
Brenda remembered those statements, but it still irritated her when
her own "baby" reminded her that what happened to Marble's son
could happen to him, too. Gerald acted as if he did not care and said,
"Mom, I'm not going to lie 'cause [Kojo] is here."

Gerald's mother wondered whether she was responsible for her
son's strong-headedness. Sometimes she speculated that perhaps she
went back to work too soon after Gerald was born (she even took a
second job when he was about two years old), which might have affected the type of person Gerald became. She blamed herself for
some of the problems of her youngest son: "Have I not been taking
enough time with him [Gerald]?" Then she suggested that perhaps
she did not spend enough time with Gerald when he was a newborn.
But she defended herself by saying that her husband was quarreling
with her, and her parents were here in Fayerville at the time and they
volunteered to take care of Gerald all the time. "Even when I wasn't
working they wouldn't let him [the baby] come to me, his mother," she
explained, showing that baby Gerald was well cared for.

Brenda was worried about the kind of company her son kept. She
did not want him to associate with men or women who were older
than he was: "I don't understand why he doesn't stay with his kind
[boys and girls his own age]." She thought that the young adults (18–

24) with whom her 16-year-old "baby" associated were not only a bad influence, but also more dangerous than his teenage peers (12–17). "He does not have a chance if something goes wrong," she feared. Even his girlfriend, a Dominican immigrant who lived in another community, was 20 years old—four years his senior. When I asked what she was going to do about it, Brenda's response was:

> I've done all I can do. I've taught him to be strong and not let anyone take advantage of him. I've shown him right from wrong [an allusion to both moral values and social norms]. I've always told him not to get involved in other people's business but to mind his own. I guess now I've got to pray that nothing happens to him.

Like most mothers in this neighborhood, Brenda blamed her son's problems—including drug activities—on others: "the wrong crowd," "wrong place," "wrong time."

On the other hand, Gerald's father seemed to hold the teenager accountable for his involvement with illegal drugs. He did not see much difference between the drug use of his son (whom he called a "crackhead") and that of his brother-in-law, Brenda's brother (whom he called a "dope fiend"). According to Ron, the only difference was that while dope fiends try to hide what they are doing from the public, crackheads are bolder and more violent. Today "nowhere is safe because of those dumb [teenage] crackheads," he said. Ron thought that children today do not care about anything and "when you don't care you have lost part of life." He said that he agreed with the motto of this neighborhood that "one should mind one's own business." However, when it involved a close relative, he felt obligated to "open my mouth and tell him." These statements by Ron were meant as criticisms of his wife's handling (or lack thereof) of her brother's (James's) and their son's (Gerald's) involvement with illegal drugs. Sandra agreed with her mother that her father's criticisms of the drug use of her mom's favorite relatives were indeed a smokescreen and that the real object of his attacks was her mother.

Gerald attributed the tension with his father to his father's disappointment that Gerald could not be coaxed into playing sports or becoming a truck driver. Gerald insisted that he would be a guitar player, and would use the money from his drug sales to buy instruments for his own band. He thought that his father's attitude reflected a characteristic problem of parents in general: wanting their children to follow in their footsteps instead of showing them how to discover what they truly would like to do with their lives. Gerald expressed this viewpoint in a simple, but poignant, manner: "They [parents] wouldn't let go of the kid." My comment that parents have more experience and want to protect their children from future hardships or mistakes provoked this quick response: "What makes the experience of parents right?" he shouted at me. I responded: "What about the old saying that experience is the best teacher?" He shot back excitedly, "Bullshit!" Then he became philosophical: "Old age doesn't [necessarily] mean wisdom or knowledge. Why are adults scared to learn from kids?" He went on, "old age has nothing to do with high IQ, some old folks don't know much, they simply are not aware. . . . To be a kid doesn't mean you're stupid." Such talk impressed friends and neighbors, who said that it reflected "deep" philosophical thinking, but his father was not impressed; he dismissed his son's statements as philosophical nonsense.

The endless tension between Ron and Gerald was a source of embarrassment for Brenda, who complained that "Ron goes about it the wrong ways. He's always accusing my baby [Gerald] of this or that . . . [and] you hate for a child to believe you always thinking something's wrong with him." However, she also admitted to being troubled by Gerald's actions: "Oh yeah! His behavior embarrasses me, sometimes. But I must honestly tell you that I'm kinda proud of him too." Sandra, the self-proclaimed Marshall family psychologist, offered the following "theory" to explain the animosity between her father and her "baby" brother. "When Gerald was little, he admired Daddy a lot and thought that he knew everything," she said. "But when he [Gerald] and my Uncle James became real tight, he began to think that Daddy may not know as much as Uncle James. . . . I think Daddy took it real hard when Gerald began to compare him to Uncle James." Furthermore, according to Sandra, things "got real bad" between her father and her brother when Gerald (at age 10) began to smoke cigarettes and drink beer. Ron Marshall wrongfully accused his son of smoking marijuana and threatened to have him put away in a reform school, but Brenda protested, "over my dead body!"

A family friend offered another explanation for the friction between Gerald and his father. She suggested that the constant fights between father and son reflected the marital problems between Brenda and Ron, which ultimately led to their separation. Like Sandra, she believed that Ron's attacks on Gerald were meant for Brenda. She also revealed that Ron had not wanted another child when Gerald was conceived and speculated that perhaps Ron suspected the baby was not his. To support her suspicion about Ron's attitude toward Gerald, she also mentioned the perennial disagreements and heated debates between Ron and Brenda's younger brother James.

STRUGGLES OF UNCLE JAMES

Besides members of his nuclear family, other relatives were influential in Gerald's life. They included his Aunt Trudy, who lived in the neighboring City of Yorkville with her family, and two uncles—James, who also lived in Fayerville, and Kenny, who lived in another state. Other collateral relatives from both sides of his family all lived in Virginia but visited occasionally. Except for his mother, Gerald was closer to his Uncle James than to any other of his many relatives.

Uncle James was three years younger than his sister Brenda was. Yet some family friends regarded them as twins because they resembled each other and were very tight while growing up. He was a veteran of the Vietnam War and worked for the United States Post Office at the time of my research. He had been separated from his wife Jackie, a friend of Brenda's, for some time as a result of his inability to keep employment due to his continuous use of illegal drugs, primarily heroin. Before securing his own apartment in the government financed, low-income housing complex popularly known as the projects, he had shared his parents' home with the Marshalls. He had to move out because Ron accused him of being a bad influence on Gerald.

Gerald admired his Uncle James because he was a "cool cat" and, above all, because he was "nonjudgmental" about other people's behavior. He was not like one of "them guys who's always telling you what's good for you, what you ought be doing, and that kinda shit. My Uncle James is not like that," Gerald assured me, "[and] that's why me and him are tight." The young nephew was obviously impressed by the depth of his uncle's knowledge. "He knows a lot, yet he never make you feel you are nothin'," Gerald said during a lengthy conversation about his relatives. The close relationship between Gerald and his Uncle James was exemplified by the fact that the teenage nephew liked to "chill" with his girlfriend in his uncle's "crib" (apartment) when James was at work and when he (Gerald) should have been in school.

Gerald's mother disapproved of her 42-year-old brother's decision to give her 16-year-old son a duplicate set of keys to his apartment. She had talked to James about this but to no avail. "Mother," Sandra pointed out to me, "is in a psychological quagmire when it comes to dealing with either Gerald or Uncle James, because besides my grandmother, they are her two most favorite relatives in our [extended] family." Indeed, it seemed that Brenda had a hard time reprimanding or chastising either James or Gerald because of her close emotional attachment to them. She explained that she could not be hard on James because he had gone through a lot of problems. He had returned from Vietnam with a dope (heroin) habit, which made it difficult for him to keep a job and eventually led him to drop out of New York University; in the middle of his struggles his wife left him and returned to Virginia with their two children. Fortunately, the therapy that James was receiving appeared to be working, and Brenda felt that he needed support, not criticism, from his family.

Dope is considered a dangerous drug by nearly 90 percent of the 39 household heads I interviewed because its use could lead a person to become a junkie, and it is commonly used intravenously, thus posing the risk of contracting HIV. Although James was a dope addict, according to the mainstream medical definition, relatives, friends, neighbors, and residents who knew him did not consider him to be a "junkie" because he came from a "good family" and had a job most of the time. In this community a "good family" means an intact family whose adult members are fully employed and have not been incarcerated. In addition, the female family members, at least, are churchgoers. On the other hand, a junkie is defined as "scum"; a lowlife; a homeless, unemployed drug addict who will steal anything from anybody—including his or her own mother—to get money to buy heroin. Junkies do this when they are experiencing withdrawal symptoms that make them uncomfortable and miserable. They are in constant pain and may have diarrhea or may be constipated. In street lingo this experience is referred to as "having the john." Preventing the onset of "the john" is therefore a major priority for every junkie.

Since James had been enrolled in a methadone maintenance program at Fayerville Hospital, he had been able to resume work at the post office uninterrupted. Almost everyone, including his nemesis Ron Marshall, blamed James's service in Vietnam for his drug addiction. According to a woman whose daughter dated James before he went to Vietnam,

> He was a very nice young man, . . . he never got himself into any trouble except, you know, he smoked reefer and drank beer like all them kids do around here [in the United States]. But when he came back from the [Vietnam] war, he was a changed man, a different person altogether. They must've done somethin' to the fine young man I knew 'cause he came back a completely changed man. He was addicted to dope [heroin] and to everything, grass, you name it. They almost ruined his life. Thank you Jesus, I hear he's on the mend and got himself a good job at the post office.

Neighborhood Griot

Gerald learned some of his philosophical rumblings from a popular neighborhood storyteller jocularly nicknamed Chickensoup. Besides his Uncle James, Gerald admired this old merchant marine and spent time listening to him retelling experiences and adventures he had all over the world. Chickensoup refused to reveal anything about his background to me. When asked how old he was, his standard reply was: "I ain't tellin'. Only my wife knows and she ain't tellin' either 'cause she passed on." It was generally assumed that he was in his late seventies.

Chickensoup's stories of adventure around the world enchanted the young men and women on his block. They appreciated his philosophy of life: let each person (young or old) learn from his or her own mistakes. Without a doubt, this former merchant marine was the hero to this neighborhood's youths. He had become a folk hero, a darling of the underdog, and Gerald and his peers were no fools: they knew that as a social group they were the underdog in U.S. society.

Chickensoup's open declaration of support for the legalization of drugs made him, in the eyes of the traditionalists in this community (that is, the church-going elderly), "a crazy old man." But the progressives (mostly young people) thought of him as a symbol or harbinger of their revolution that was yet to come. He had been variously described as an "honest man," "ahead of his time," and, in the words of a local activist, "a genius of common sense." On the other hand, he had been called a "lunatic," "evil," "con man," and a "dangerous old man" because of his chronic use of the marijuana that he swore had medicinal properties. Because of this, and also because his deceased wife was from the Island of Dominica, some people speculated that Chickensoup might be a West Indian. His response was always the same: that he was an African. He referred to Black people everywhere as Africans.

I wanted to discuss Gerald's involvement with illegal drugs with Chickensoup, but he wouldn't talk about the specifics of Gerald's or any of the other youths' involvement with illegal drugs. However, he was eager to criticize the United States government's drug policies. He articulated what many adults in this neighborhood said to me in private but seldom admitted in public. "It's difficult to tell a kid with $200–$300 in his pocket that he is in the wrong business," he said with a chuckle.

PATTERN OF DRUG INVOLVEMENT

Gerald told me that he had experimented with crack, cocaine, angel dust, and heroin, but used marijuana, which he called "buddha," on a regular basis. He smoked three or four times a day. He also sold these drugs, primarily in Southland, but also in the neighboring metropolis of Central City. Gerald began his involvement with illegal drugs at the youthful age of twelve. He acted as a lookout for the older boys on his block who actually sold the drugs. Gerald and his friends, Anthony and Tyrone, were each given ten dollars a week for warning the older boys when the police were approaching. They would stand at the entrance to their block and when they saw a patrol car preparing to turn onto their street, they either whistled or gave a sign to alert the drug dealers.

Gerald had an opportunity to work at the local McDonald's, but like most teenagers with whom I spoke in this community, he turned it down (c.f., Newman 1999). Gerald said that he wanted to become his own man so that he did not have to take orders from anyone. He related this desire to an incident that occurred when he was just 10 years old. He wanted to work for tips as a bagger at a Waldbaum's supermarket on the Northside of town, but the manager would not allow him to do so because, according to the manager, customers (most of whom were White) complained about the Black boys stealing some of the groceries that they bagged and helped to carry to customers' cars. Gerald accused this manager of being a racist and he later claimed that he was not treated fairly because he was Black and lived in Southland. He said that the manager had assumed that he was a "drug dealer."[1] According to Sandra, the experience had such an impact on her younger brother that he had stopped trying to look for legitimate employment and, instead, began to work as a lookout for the "big" boys on his block. Gerald's childhood friend, Tyrone, disagreed with this version of events and claimed that he and Gerald were already working as lookouts, although prior to this episode they were not getting paid. He said that initially they did it for the thrill and also because the older boys they helped were all known to them as "big brothers."

In any case, Gerald eventually decided to become his "own man," that is, an independent drug peddler, because he felt that the older boys were cheating him and his friends, giving them "peanuts." He knew where they got their supplies; he knew the friends of his Uncle James and of his older brothers who supplied the bigger boys on his block. To purchase his initial drug supplies, he needed "dividends" (seed money or capital), so he began concocting stories that enabled him to get the money from his mother or borrow it from his sister. By the time he turned 15, when the judge threatened to send him away, he was making a profit of $300–$400 a week. He mainly sold dope, crack, cocaine, angel dust, and marijuana, but he did not sell these drugs all the time. Rather he was a part-time dealer, who peddled drugs only when he needed money badly. According to Gerald, this was a merchandising strategy to mislead the cops. However, it might also be due to pressure put on him by his relatives, particularly by his father, who continued to reprimand him.

Gerald maintained that he did not sell dope to "kids" (teenagers), but only to adults (over the age of 25). I asked him if he was concerned about selling dope to people whom he knew might use dirty needles to shoot the drug. His emphatic answer was: "Hell no! If they want to get AIDS and die it's none of my business." Like many of his peers, Gerald tried to project the "macho image" most of the time by talking tough. He went on to say that if drug addicts or junkies want to die, he would help sell them drugs to ease the exit from this world. This is how he put it: "the junkies who want to die can put five [dollars] in my pocket, and I'll help them make it out [of here] with a smile and one on my face too."

Gerald also told me that he would not, however, sell heroin to kids. When I asked him why he would not sell dope to young people even though he was willing to sell them crack, he defended his stance on selling crack,

> What the hell you want from me? If a kid wants to kill himself in his own way, what can I do about it? There is nothing you or me can do about it. This is a free country, right? If the kid ain't got a job or nothing to do, he may as well smoke the pipe. . . . Let him hold up his mama to keep with his habit so long as he don't hold me up or my mother. If one of them lays his hand on my mother or my sister, I will kill him quicker than the pipe.

Then I asked him if there was anything else (beside not selling heroin to kids) he would not do. Without hesitation Gerald said that he would not encourage five- or six-year-olds to collect and sell empty crack vials. He was referring to the practice of crack dealers encouraging little children to collect old, used crack vials in exchange for money—a quarter for a vial, which is more than collecting the deposit on cans or bottles. Gerald laughed at my ironic suggestion that this practice served the useful purpose of recycling. He disagreed and called the practice "dangerous" because it could make children targets of rival crack dealers.

Gerald's responses and the image he was trying to project need to be viewed in the context of the social norms of the Southland neighborhood as they relate to young people. His strategy of not appearing as a "sucker" or a "softie" included, among other things, sharing joints with both friends and acquaintances. He said that it was not simply trying to appear cool but also projecting an image of toughness. "I smoke what older people say kids shouldn't touch [marijuana laced with cocaine]," he once said proudly. It was important to him that he not be considered a sucker or a softie because a sucker is often the target of unprovoked assaults, and other youths will take advantage of him. Smoking "buddha" or a blunt symbolizes that a 16-year-old is no longer a "kid," but a young adult.

THE MAN OF THE HOUSE

After dropping out of school, Gerald's daily routine changed drastically. His day began late, after 11:00 A.M., because he went to bed in the wee hours of the morning. He did not always sleep at his home. He slept at his uncle's place when James traveled to Virginia to see his children. On those occasions, Gerald invited his girlfriend, Lourdes, who lived in an adjacent neighborhood of Central City, to join him. Regardless of the time he awoke, Gerald began his day with breakfast (pancakes and either cereal or grits, toast, home fries, and sausage, always accompanied by orange juice and coffee). There was a tradition in his family of the men eating breakfast outside the home, in one of the local eateries. The women, on the other hand, ate breakfast at home, except when they had to go to work early in the morning. No one knew how this tradition began or who started it. Brenda said that when her husband came along he, too, would not eat breakfast at home. "All my boys straight on up to their grandfather like to eat breakfast outside," she said with a puzzled look on her face. Sandra thought it was a macho thing that her grandfather began.

But even though the big sign at the entrance to the Yankee Cafe, Gerald's favorite eatery, reads, "breakfast served from 6:00 A.M. to 11:00 A.M.," Delores, the 50-year-old waitress, still served him breakfast after 11:00 A.M. When I asked Delores why she served Gerald breakfast so late, she said that she had known Gerald since he was a little boy, when he came in with his grandfather, and she added, "Am I to leave him starving?" The same waitress, when Gerald was not around, referred to this 16-year-old "problem kid" as a gentleman. This prompted me to ask her about his drug activities. Her quick response was: "All the kids today do drugs, they sell, they use them, so what you gonna do? It's a shame because it starts at home, and I know his family. They are the nicest people you'll wanna meet." She denied that her kind words about Gerald and his family had anything to do with the fact that this teenager often left her a five-dollar tip. Instead she argued that his generosity confirmed her impression of him as a gentleman. Indeed, 16-year-old Gerald was often regarded by people as a "miniature adult."

The characterization "miniature adult" refers to Black youths who take on adult responsibilities because one of their parents (often the father) is not around. Since his father, older brothers, and Uncle James had moved away from home, Gerald had become the de facto "man of the house," although his mother ran the household. I asked Delores, who seemed to have known Gerald's extended family for almost three decades, about Gerald's social position within the household. I was intrigued by her reference to this 16-year-old as "the man of the house," so I asked her about Ron, Gerald's father, who after all had lived with his family for over 20 years. Her response was that Ron had been a good family man who tried to provide for his family, but he could not have been considered the man of the house. "What do you mean?" I said before she could finish what she was saying. "That's not his house," she intoned with the confidence of an insider. She implored me to ask around.

Indeed, neighbors who knew the Marshall family very well agreed with the waitress's observation and analysis. They pointed out to me that it was difficult to consider Ron the "man of the house" when he lived in a house owned by his in-laws. Even though Brenda and Ron were asked to assume the remaining mortgage payments when her parents moved back to Virginia, Brenda alone paid them in order to maintain the title in her maiden name. This was also another source of conflict in the marriage between Ron and Brenda. However, Ron seemed to have accepted the arrangement over the years in order to maintain tranquil relations in the household. Delores told me that Brenda's younger brother James could have succeeded his father as "the man of that house," but his drug abuse problem, which led to the break-up of his marriage, seemed to have "destroyed" any chance of that. She said that Gerald showed signs that he was ready to assume the mantel of his grandfather and that the old man was pleased with him as his successor.

Gerald did not talk about usurping the authority of his father, but he acted as if he was the man of the house and both his older sister and mother perceived him as such. The proceeds from his drug sales enabled him to fulfill the financial obligations that came with his role as man of the house. Even though he did not watch television often, Gerald had cable installed (and paid the monthly fees) because his mother, sister, and niece liked to watch television. When Gerald watched television he preferred just two stations: Black Entertainment Television (BET) and Music Television (MTV). Brenda knew that Gerald did not have a regular job, yet she did not question him about where he got the money to pay the monthly cable fees. In the prevailing circumstances, it was not clear to me who was the actual household head.

Besides selling drugs, however, Gerald was sporadically employed doing odd jobs, such as helping to repair homes or hauling furniture from one location to another. He did these temporary jobs when he was short of cash. He worked for subcontractors off the books, so that no taxes would be deducted from his wages. This deprived him of any benefits, which he said he did not need because both of his parents worked. This pattern of work is adaptive to the circumstances of the inner-city neighborhood (Anderson 1980) and is adopted by many of the chronically unemployed young men in this neighborhood.

MAKING HIS OWN CHOICES

Gerald perceived drug dealing as a "dead man's game" because it engenders violence, which more often than not, results in killings. He explained:

> The money you make makes you immediately a target of robbers. The robbery is likely to be committed by your friends or by those who know you, unless you are willing to dish it [money] out freely like a godfather to others. If robbers don't get you, the police will eventually catch up with you. Either way you are likely to get killed.

If drug dealing can lead to violent death, why did Gerald continue to deal drugs? He explained that he did it to raise money to buy instruments for his own band. Gerald said that he was tired of people telling him what to do when "what I really like to do is playing bass guitar. . . ." He resented it when people talked about his guitar playing as if it were not hard work. He insisted that as soon as he had made enough money to buy the instruments, he would turn to "legit" business and become a recording artist. He said that his Uncle James told him that Joseph Kennedy, the father of President John F. Kennedy, was a bootlegger during prohibition and that he used profits from that business to invest on Wall Street. He also observed that most working adults he knew hated their jobs. A neighbor who had worked as a secretary for nearly a decade complained, "I only do it to take care of my kids. If I had no kids I won't be doing this kind of work. I'd be singing full-time . . . that's what I enjoy." Another neighbor, Mr. Johnson, hated his work as a clerk in the drug store, even though he made a decent wage. He told young Gerald that if he could have afforded it, he would have become a professional artist.

These are just two of many adult neighbors with whom Gerald interacted on a fairly regular basis. They had seen and heard Gerald play the guitar and thought he was talented. Indeed, Gerald was an accomplished musician already, for he had written a few songs that had been made into CDs, but they were poorly promoted so he had not made any money. He had been looking for a recording contract, which usually required sponsorship. However, Gerald intended to create his own "seed money" instead of searching for a White or corporate sponsor. His mother had been very supportive, giving him money when she could.

Brenda's efforts to encourage Gerald to develop his musical talent, however, brought her into conflict with her husband, who did not think highly of musicians. "What has music brought the Black man?" he asked disdainfully. "Nothin' but the blues!" He said that Black folks' legendary interest in religion and the church was simply an extension of their love affair with music and their desire, during slavery, for life after death. He agreed with Gerald that "music is the dope of Black people," but he blamed this cultural addiction to music on the lack of economic advancement facing so many Blacks. He believed that Blacks had not made economic strides comparable to their strides in politics because most were consumed by "this nonsense about music and religion." He vehemently opposed his son's ambition to become a musician, but he did not oppose his desire to be a music producer because that was business—hard work—as he saw it.

In spite of his awareness that drug dealing often led to quick death, Gerald had no plans to quit any time soon. As he characteristically put it, "When your time is up, there's nothing you can do about it." He had seen a few of his peers and the older boys on his block gunned down. But he denied wanting to become a "big time" drug dealer, noting that if he had wanted to become a big time drug dealer, he would have moved to Atlanta, Georgia, or Norfolk, Virginia.

Uncle James did not consider his nephew to be a drug dealer, either. He also denied that Gerald was a drug addict, because he primarily smoked marijuana. According to James, "One cannot be addicted to marijuana unless the concept of addiction is so broadly defined as to make its usage almost useless." According to James, drug dealers are like managers whose business is to plan how to control both drug pushers and users, as well as anyone who might interfere with their drug operations (i.e., police officers, as well as parents or guardians). According to James, "Gerald is a pusher, that's what he is, a natural-born pusher." And what is a pusher? I asked.

> I'll tell you what a pusher is, but first you must forget about what's written in your textbooks. A pusher is nothing but a salesman, no matter what he's selling. The commercials you see on television are being pushed by salesmen who tell you to run out and buy cars, beer, shoes, clothes, or whatever they can talk you into buying. Gerald is nothin' but a salesman, a pusher. As simple as that.

Why wouldn't this young "salesman" finish high school? Gerald gave convoluted but revealing reasons why he had dropped out of high school. His persistent truancy led to his transfer from Fayerville High School to Fayerville Academy (later renamed Pan-African High School), an alternative school for "disruptive" students. He said that he would not attend Pan-African High School because of the school's stigma as a dump for special education students, that is, "dummies," and that he was not a "dummy." He said that when he was serious about school he received A's and B's, and the only time he received a C was after he had lost interest and no longer took school seriously.

Gerald denied that the decline of his interest in school had anything to do with drugs, as his mother suspected. Rather, he explained that he had already received enough education to function in American society. He had begun to feel that Fayerville High School was like a prison, a place of punishment, and not a place of learning, inspiring youngsters to develop their talents. To underscore this point, he bluntly stated:

> I hate school and that's why I stopped going. . . . [I] hang out with those who hate the school too. Going to school is a waste of time

Gerald by His Own Bootstraps

'cause you there for studying nothin'. The math they teach you will not help you later in life. All you need to know is how to read and count and I already know how to do that. I don't know how to count to a billion but I don't have to worry 'cause I will not have a billion dollars anyway.

On another occasion, when the subject of education was brought up, Gerald implied that he dropped out because he found classes boring. This time his complaint was that many teachers in Fayerville High School "do not care about us [students]" and no amount of pretense was going to change his lack of faith in them. About his mother's hope that he, too, would attend college as his older siblings did, he blurted out, "Why must I go to college, tell me, why?" When I suggested to him, "Won't you want to be a lawyer, a doctor, or an astronaut?" he responded emphatically "Nope!" He defiantly added, "I want none of that. I want [to] be me, Gerald . . . I already told you, what I wanna do with my life. I want to be a recording artist, a guitar player, and a music producer." Again, he insisted that he wanted to be his own man, that he did not need anyone telling him when to go to work and what he should or could not do. He ended his statement with an emphatic, "I want none of that!", referring to the middle-class notion of a career. Gerald wanted to work for himself and, if necessary, to employ others to work for him.

Brenda had talked Gerald into attending counseling at the Drug Treatment Center on South Sixth Avenue. He went to a few sessions and then stopped, explaining that the counselors were forcing him to become someone else; he wanted to be himself, not what his mother or anybody else wanted him to be. He insisted that he did not need any structures (such as boot camps or therapeutic communities); he wanted a job where he could make his own hours. He believed in himself and, although he was good at fixing televisions or radios, what he liked most was playing bass guitar in a band.

Gerald felt that his mother "[got] on his case" because he had stopped going to school, not because he smoked blunts or sold drugs. He believed that his involvement with drugs was less of a problem than his refusal to act according to the expectations of his parents, that is, to take an interest in sports or academic subjects. When I asked him whether he thought his behavior might be influenced by his smoking marijuana, he smiled, looked up, then said, "You really want to know the truth? As far as I'm concerned drugs ain't the cause of nobody's problems." Even if drugs were harmful, Gerald said, the government should allow adults to use them if they so desire. An "adult" in one context meant someone over the age 21, at other times, it referred to someone 25 or above. During this particular conversation, Gerald seemed to suggest that anyone in this neighborhood 12 years old or older was an adult because persons that age were "street smart."

Conclusion

The portrait of Gerald debunks the myths that inner-city Black youths who sell and/or use illegal drugs come from dysfunctional families and reveals that illegal drugs are integrated into the daily lives of ordinary residents of Southland. In the Marshall household, every member except Keisha, Sandra's little girl, had experimented with smoking marijuana. This did not prevent neighbors from regarding them as a good family. Even though some labeled Gerald a "problem kid," the label had referred to being arrested for offenses other than involvement with illegal drugs. Gerald was well-liked by many residents of this community because of his family ties, and they also respected the 16-year-old as a "miniature adult." They recognized that he had become the de facto "man of the house." The reporter who wrote about Gerald in the now-defunct local newspaper said that what prompted him to focus on Gerald was that he did not fit the profile of familiar images of Black youths whose ruined lives cried out for sympathy.

Selling drugs was one of the many jobs Gerald did to earn money, as many people did in Southland. Occupational multiplicity does not occur only in third-world rural economies (Comitas 1973), but also in depressed inner-city economies as well as in some U.S. rural areas. Gerald, like most residents, was always thinking about making money. He saw retailing drugs as another opportunity to make money, which allowed him to do things his way and on his own terms. Compromise was not in his vocabulary, because compromises were seen as a sign of weakness. While income from drug sales was earmarked for the purchase of musical instruments, it also enabled Gerald to fulfill the role of man of the house. One way he demonstrated this role was by giving his mother, sister, and niece money without their asking him about its source.

The Southland community does not regard all illegal drugs as dangerous, nor does it uncritically condemn all persons who are involved with drugs. Drug dealers and drug users are not the focus of the community's concern. Gerald's portrait shows that family dynamics are intertwined with the use and sale of illegal drugs and that drugs have symbolic, as well as physical, emotional, and economic implications.

NOTE

[1] Children as young as five have been caught delivering marijuana to customers.

CHAPTER 4

Akosua's Ties That Bind

Akosua is the pseudonym of a young African-American woman I first met in the spring of 1990.[1] Her real name was the same as a very popular African political leader. It was chosen by Akosua's parents because she was born in 1970 during the period of Black power struggles when African Americans proudly tried to reclaim their African heritage through adoption of African clothing and African names. Akosua did so much to open the world of young African-American women to me in a fashion unmatched by any informant I had during the entire period of my fieldwork in Southland. She was simply my principal source of information, my first and foremost informant.

Akosua was a very thoughtful, outgoing, highly intelligent, and an insightful person. She could, however, also be very stubborn, withdrawn, uncooperative, and at times stoic, if she chose not to cooperate. Even though she liked to assert her rights as an independent person, she was not a particularly "liberated" woman as many young women were these days; some of her values were very traditional. For example, she said that no woman should become a mother if she had no husband and counseled young women against becoming mothers when they weren't ready. Her behavior and attitude were highly complex, and she could not be fitted easily into a predetermined category because she straddled two cultures—her own African-American culture and that of the dominant White middle class.

Akosua, now a mother of two little boys, was five months pregnant with her second child when we first met. She lived with her husband, an ex-convict and a well-known local drug dealer, in a homeless shelter. She attended College Opportunities, Inc., one of the two alternative high schools located in Southland. In many ways Akosua was like the other students, but she was different in some significant ways too. For example, almost all of her classmates at College Opportunities, Inc., had been convicted of drug-related crimes and had been mandated to attend this alternative school by the courts in lieu of a prison sentence, or they were there because the probation department ordered them to enroll in the program. Akosua, who had dropped out of Fayerville High School at the start of the eleventh grade even though she had a B+ average and was well liked by her teachers, was not under such a court mandate because, even though she used and sold drugs, she had so far managed to escape arrest. It was unusual for students to enroll voluntarily in an alternative school program, and therefore it was rumored that Akosua was in the program for the money. As an incentive, this privately sponsored program paid each student who attended classes regularly and did all the assignments a weekly stipend of $18. Akosua denied that she was motivated by the money and insisted that she returned to school to prepare and sit for the General Equivalency Diploma (GED) in order to attend college.

Another difference between Akosua and her fellow students was that, unlike the others, Akosua was an avid reader who regularly visited the Fayerville Public Library. Her possession of a library card significantly distinguished her from her peers and neighbors in the homeless shelter. Akosua wanted to attend college and major in English, for her ambition was to become a writer of children's books. Akosua's love of books and her general intellectual curiosity, more than anything else, distinguished her from the other students at this alternative school.

SOCIAL RELATIONSHIPS

How did it happen that this bright, promising, young woman became involved with illegal drugs and eventually dropped out of high school? Both of Akosua's parents had been killed in tragic circumstances.

When she was four years old, her father was murdered while vacationing in his home state of North Carolina; two years later her mother, too, was murdered by a man she had begun to date following her husband's death. So Akosua grew up in the household of her maternal relatives who cared for her and her younger brother Kwame,[2] who was in prison during the period of my fieldwork. The household head was her grandmother (whom Akosua called "Granny"). As a result of the untimely death of her father, Akosua grew up having little contact with her paternal relatives, except her father's mother, whom she called Grandma to differentiate her from Granny, and with whom she lived briefly after dropping out of high school.

Also living in the household where Akosua grew up was her mother's older sister, Terry, who became her legal guardian after Granny passed away (when Akosua was 11 years old). Aunt Terry lived with her son, Marc, who returned from military duty in Vietnam addicted to heroin and filled with hatred toward the United States government. In the same household was also Akosua's Uncle David, who spent more time in the penitentiary than he did at home, and who now suffers from chronic alcoholism, which has damaged his liver. Another member of Akosua's household (though not a relative) was a West Indian immigrant known as Mr. Thomas. He rented a room on the second floor of the two-family house. Akosua had other relatives who lived in the neighboring metropolis of Central City and in North Carolina, but they all seemed to have little or no influence on her, since she did not interact with them on a regular basis. Perhaps her Aunt Shirley, who lived close to Southland in Bloomfield, a borough of Central City, was an exception because she tried (without success) to keep an eye on her niece.

Although heroin was readily available in the neighborhood (Southland), Akosua grew up on marijuana (reefer), which was the common drug of choice. All the adult members of Akosua's household, as well as neighbors whose homes she visited almost daily, smoked marijuana. For example, Granny, the household matriarch, smoked reefer almost every day. According to Akosua, on those occasions when Granny smoked alone, she would ask Akosua to roll the reefer into joints for her, but "she did not allow me to taste the smoke because she said I was too young." Aunt Terry confirmed this and added that, as a young woman, she and Akosua's mother used to smoke reefer together, but rarely did they involve Akosua or her younger brother Kwame. She also maintained that Akosua's mother was not a regular smoker and did not smoke reefer by herself.

Aunt Terry, on the other hand, was a regular marijuana smoker like her mother (Granny); she smoked and drank until quite recently. At the time of the research she had given up smoking and drinking because, as she put it, "the older you get the more you realize that your body is tired of them things [implying drugs and alcohol, as well as unrestrained sexual activities]." Aunt Terry's attempt to imply that she gave up drugs of her own volition is not quite accurate. However, ever since Marc became a Black Muslim in prison, she has become sympathetic toward the religious and political movement of the Black Muslims, one of a few institutions that have taken an unequivocal stance against drug and alcohol use in predominantly low-income neighborhoods throughout this nation. According to Akosua, both her Cousin Marc and her Uncle David smoked reefer and used "dope" (heroin), yet she referred only to David as the "real" drug addict in her Granny's house.

Neighbors explained that Uncle David was "the black sheep of the family [implying Akosua's household]." He abused both drugs and alcohol and was in and out of rehabs as well as jail. He used to shoot dope but had stopped for fear of HIV infection. Still, "he's married to the pipe," as Akosua eloquently described her Uncle David's latest addiction to crack. Finally, the West Indian boarder in Granny's house, Mr. Thomas, smoked marijuana and drank a substantial amount of rum on weekends. Thus, all the immediate relatives or adult household members with whom Akosua lived and interacted intensely on a daily basis used at least one illegal drug—marijuana.

Marijuana has been readily available in Fayerville since the 1960s. Aunt Terry, for example, remembered using marijuana occasionally before Akosua was born. Even though she did not ask Akosua to roll her marijuana into cigarettes for her as Granny did, she nevertheless did send Akosua, who was nine or ten years old at the time, to pick up her purchases from a neighbor. Granny's source of her marijuana supply was her estranged husband, who lived in Green Meadows.

Akosua said that by the age of six or seven, she understood that reefer made Granny feel "relaxed," Aunt Terry feel "horny," Cousin Marc become "argumentative," Uncle David get "high," Mr. Thomas become "boisterous," and Grandpa Willie (Granny's estranged husband) "calm down." Akosua's description of the effects of marijuana smoking confirms what Howard Becker found in his studies of not only marijuana but other illegal drugs as well: that drugs have multifarious effects, and that users learn to focus on the "beneficial" effects while ignoring those effects deemed irrelevant to the benefit they seek (1986a:45).

I questioned Aunt Terry about whether she thought her own drug use might have influenced her niece's later involvement with illegal drugs. She appeared unconvinced that it had, although she did not deny sending Akosua to pick up a bag or two of marijuana for her "on a few occasions." She did not feel responsible for Akosua's drug career, however. Aunt Terry swore that Akosua had experimented with marijuana before she became Akosua's guardian. She maintained that the "little girl" began to experiment with reefer during a brief stay in Green Meadows. Immediately following the murder of Akosua's mother, Granny had moved her grandchildren from Fayerville to Green Meadows, where her estranged husband was living. Within 15 months, she too passed away, prompting Akosua and her brother to return to Southland, where they were placed in the custody of their Aunt Terry.

Besides, Aunt Terry argued, "reefer is no more dangerous than cigarettes or booze." Indeed, like many residents in the Southland, Aunt Terry believed that marijuana was less harmful than alcohol. A 43-year-old neighbor of Aunt Terry said: "Give me reefer a hundred times before I will touch booze. Alcohol is the real killer. . . . I've been smoking [marijuana] for 25 years and nothing has happened to me."

Although Akosua became an orphan at the early age of six, Aunt Terry claimed to have always loved and supported her. Neighbors confirmed this, saying; "She [Akosua] was the daughter Ms. Terry never had." Aunt Terry told me that following the death of her sister, she and Granny were determined to do everything possible to make Akosua and Kwame feel that they were loved, wanted, and cared for. Akosua agreed with this assessment of the situation and described the relationship she had with Aunt Terry at that time in glowing terms:

> When I was coming up she [Aunt Terry] was my idol, the most wonderful person in the world. I wanted to grow up just like her, beautiful, wearing nice clothes. Sophisticated. Won't let nobody tell me what to do. . . . My aunt loved kids, she played with us [Akosua and Kwame] and took us out all the time. When we came back home, she would bake cookies for us, . . . [and although] she did not go school [beyond] sixth grade, she liked to read to us.

However, when Akosua was 13 or 14 years old, her feelings toward her aunt changed. She even accused her of being greedy and becoming her guardian so that she could collect Aid for Families with Dependent Children (AFDC) to buy drugs, clothes, and jewelry for herself. Akosua now says that her "problems" with Aunt Terry at the

time contributed to her eloping to get married earlier than she would
have. Furthermore, Akosua now admits that it would have been better
to finish college before getting married, as her Aunt Terry had tried
but failed to persuade her to do.

Aunt Margaret, a friend of Akosua's deceased mother, was a keen
observer of the drama unfolding in Akosua's maternal home. She said
that she was aware of Akosua's early experiments with marijuana and
occasional youthful binge drinking. But, like most other people in this
community, she did not want to say anything about it to Aunt Terry or
any of Akosua's relatives because of the problems it might have
caused Akosua and perhaps herself. When I insisted on asking her
further questions about her reluctance to alert Akosua's relatives, she
blurted out:

> It's really none of my business! . . . The little girl has become a
> young woman but did not have a lip like some of them. She was
> always polite to me, so why get her and myself into trouble?
> Where I come from, when a child did something wrong like that
> you could talk to her, but here they may curse and threaten you.

Even though excessive drinking and smoking reefer are not uncommon in this community, senior citizens as well as middle-aged
women like Aunt Margaret tended to express disapproval of "little
girls" (i.e., young women) drinking too much or smoking reefer.
When Akosua began to experiment with drugs, Aunt Terry was "wag-
ing her own [battle] to stop smoking and drinking." She did not condemn Akosua's behavior outright, but instead warned her about the
difficulty in quitting once "you get hooked." Akosua did not take her
Aunt Terry's warning seriously, dismissing it as pro forma advice or a
scare tactic. This type of contradictory behavior or ambivalence on the
part of Aunt Terry and other adults leads young people in this community, like Akosua, to believe the adults are hypocrites.

As neighbors talked about the soured relationship between Akosua and Aunt Terry, they stressed the differences between Aunt Terry
and her deceased sister, Akosua's mother. They expressed how pain-
ful it might be for Aunt Terry because "she raised that child . . . [even]
when her mother was alive." Aunt Margaret, for example, told me that
Akosua's mother Joyce did not want children, and her two children
were not planned; "she had them by accident." She said further that
Joyce often left her children to be cared for by her older sister, Terry,
or her mother (Granny).

Becoming Independent

Akosua had begun to cut classes in the tenth grade, although she managed to complete that academic year successfully. She would leave home saying that she was going to school, but instead she went with other girls to the mall in Green Meadows or took the subway to Central City. Gradually, her enthusiasm for school began to wane, and in the eleventh grade she quit completely. Around this time she began what became her only serious relationship with a young man besides her husband Jimmy. This young man's name was Francis, and his parents were from St. Lucia in the West Indies. Akosua says that she was "madly" in love with him. Her devotion to him had the effect of lowering all the inhibitions that this "shy, pretty, little girl" had. Francis taught Akosua how to freebase cocaine and influenced her to become a petty thief.

When Akosua dropped out of Fayerville High School, she also moved out of the home in which she grew up, and thus symbolically rejected the authority of her guardian, Aunt Terry, who was surprised and devastated when her niece decided to quit school. But it was no surprise to her neighbors, who knew that Akosua—like their own children—had been cutting classes or "playing hooky," as they say on the streets. One neighbor expressed disbelief that Aunt Terry was not aware of what was going on with her niece because, as she pointed out, "we all get letters from the principal when our kids been missing from school." Aunt Margaret, who knew Akosua's family well, explained that Aunt Terry might not have been completely aware of what was going on because she had been distraught over the years following the murder of her sister (Akosua's mother), the sudden death of her mother (Granny), and the murder conviction of her son Marc. Aunt Margaret thinks that these misfortunes influenced Aunt Terry "to drink a lot and smoke reefer to cope."

When Akosua moved out of her aunt's house, she went to stay with her paternal grandmother (known to her as "Grandma"). For Akosua, the change of address, as well as the change in kinship alliance, signaled her own coming of age. As she explained, "I wanted to be independent, to take care of me first." She found employment as a sales clerk in neighboring Yorkville. But her aspiration of becoming a self-sufficient working woman did not last long. Within a year she was dismissed (following a warning) for stealing an expensive shirt that she told me she wanted to give to her boyfriend as a birthday present. This was Akosua's first brush with the law, so she was given only probation. However, more troubling times lay ahead of her. Grandma's eyesight had deteriorated so badly that she decided to move to a nursing home, where professional staff could give her assistance when she needed it. Grandma's decision forced Akosua to seek refuge with her boyfriend's cousin, Judy. Akosua did not want to return to her natal home because she had grown distant from her Aunt Terry, who headed that household.

Judy was a 30-year-old drug abuser with a reputation as a "trick" (prostitute). However, Akosua claimed that this did not bother her because she was "not going to be like that"; she liked Judy because Judy treated her fairly as an adult. After moving in with Judy, Akosua began to smoke crack regularly, four or five times a week. Asked to describe her experience with crack, Akosua said: "It doesn't make me wanna go out and whore around or anything like that. If it's around I want some to smoke; if it's not available it doesn't bother me. Crack doesn't do much for me anyway, except keep me up all night." It was in Judy's "crib" that she tried reefer sprinkled with angel dust, and found it to be "dangerous."

Akosua worked briefly as a cashier in a local supermarket, earning the minimum wage at that time—$4.25 an hour. Her income was not enough to cover her share of the expenses with Judy, but she did not want to seek financial support from relatives or friends. So she made a critical decision to sell small quantities of marijuana, cocaine, and crack, which were given to her by one of Francis's friends to help her out (Francis was in jail at this time). She sold the drugs to her coworkers and to other people she knew as acquaintances; she did not, however, sell to friends. Akosua believes that this strategy is what kept her from being arrested on drug possession charges. As she put it, "when people get greedy, they'll sell to anybody. That's how they get arrested. I never do that. I'm not a greedy person." Here, she meant to say that there are three types of customers—friends, acquaintances, and strangers. She believed that it is safest to sell only to acquaintances. Peddling drugs influenced Akosua to hang out on the streets, and she now spent more time on street corners than before. She denied that she ever exchanged sex for drugs.

Although Akosua did not want to admit it, others, including her best friend Regina (of whom we will hear more later), said that Judy influenced her decisions in important ways. For instance, they said that she encouraged Akosua to spend more time on the streets, which kept her away from her relatives and friends. According to Regina, who had known Akosua for many years,

> Akosua wasn't like that, she never did like street life, she was scared of all the things that went on in the streets. That's how she and I became friends. We were neighbors and we enjoyed sitting on the stoop and watching the world go by instead of hanging out on the streets and [perhaps] getting our heads blown off. We have fun at home. Talking, listening to music, that kinda thin'. . . . Akosua like to read and cook, so we ate a lot, . . . but after she disappeared with Judy, I didn't know what was goin' on 'cause she wouldn't come around and didn't call me much.

MARRIAGE TO JIMMY

Thirty-three-year-old Jimmy and 20-year-old Akosua had been married for almost two years when I met them. They had two young boys (PJ, who was two, and Shawn, who was born during my fieldwork). Akosua had known Jimmy since she was a little girl, but she insisted that "we was not dating or anything like that." Indeed, they dated for a brief period (a couple of months); then they eloped to get married soon after Akosua turned eighteen. Aunt Terry maintains that it was because of the disparity in age that she disapproved of Akosua's marriage to Jimmy. However, on another occasion, I heard her say that a student as smart as Akosua should have completed college before getting married. In any event, her disapproval did not prevent Akosua, who described herself as "a very stubborn woman," from going ahead and secretly marrying Jimmy. Aunt Terry recalled her utter disappointment: "I was there for her like a mother, a sister, a friend, until I realized that I had lost [the battle], that the little girl was now a young woman, and the young woman had chosen Jimmy as her savior."

Akosua's consanguineal relatives withheld their support for her marriage to Jimmy for other reasons as well. Jimmy had just been released from prison after serving a three-year sentence on a drug-related conviction. He was not working, and employment prospects for a Black male dropout with a long "rap sheet" were not good, even though he had earned his GED during his incarceration. Dropping out of school and getting married without stable employment possibilities concerned almost every mother, sister, or girlfriend in the Southland, and these concerns certainly did not escape Aunt Terry when her niece broached the subject of marrying Jimmy. "How you all goin' support yourself?" she shouted. "Him being on welfare and you, too, on welfare. That's no way to start a family," she warned Akosua, but the young woman did not listen.

Akosua knew that what she intended to do was not unheard of. In fact, scores of young women in her community, including members of her own family, had made similar choices. She knew it probably would have been better to finish college before getting married. However, she assured herself that it was no big deal if she got married and then went to college later or didn't even go to college at all. In middle-class households such thoughts may be unacceptable, but in working-class homes such thoughts are not uncommon. Perhaps among middle-class families the choice of marrying an unemployed, uneducated ex-convict may be perceived as a zero sum game, however, in Southland this is not necessarily the case.

According to Akosua, Jimmy "had given up drugs when he came in contact with the [Black] Muslims in prison." However, Jimmy was not a practicing Muslim or a follower of Islam, but like many young Black men without any developed skills or a recognized career, he sympathized with this politico-religious movement. Also, it should be noted that Jimmy refused to talk to me, despite my repeated requests. Thus, the information about him is based on what Akosua and others told me. Jimmy even tried to dissuade Akosua from cooperating with me, but she resisted.

Since Jimmy's drug-dealing days were supposedly over, he and Akosua had no regular source of income other than public assistance. It is difficult to say whether Jimmy's decision not to resume drug dealing was due to a fundamental change in his attitude toward drugs or simply to the fact that he was on parole following his release from prison and thus obliged to refrain from involvement with illegal drugs. Besides, although he was no longer dealing (or doing drugs), he had begun to drink heavily. It got to the point that his social worker and probation officer urged him to join Alcoholics Anonymous (AA). Apparently, it was attending AA meetings that enabled Jimmy to receive welfare checks past the eligibility period of six months after his release from prison.

Why did Akosua, a young, attractive, and talented woman, decide to marry Jimmy, a man with a long rap sheet and no reliable source of income? She maintained that she agreed to marry Jimmy because "he was the one who got my mind straight [i.e., away from crack], and I just fell in love with him for that." However, Regina was of the opinion that Jimmy "tricked" Akosua with promises of relocating and starting a family in California, where he claimed to have money stashed away.

While Akosua grew up in a household full of adults who smoked reefer, Jimmy, the youngest of seven children, grew up with older siblings who used and sold all types of illicit drugs, including marijuana, heroin, cocaine, crack, pills (barbiturates), angel dust, and LSD. Jimmy began his drug career in his preteens as a look out. By age 14 he was a pusher, and a few years later he controlled some of the street peddlers on Wayward Street, thus becoming a local drug kingpin of sorts. By the time he turned 18, he had become a drug dealer "big time," as they say on the streets. He had been arrested a few times and had spent short terms in jail before he was sent to prison for eight years but served only three years.

Akosua remembered Jimmy before his incarceration as "a generous man who gave me money to go buy something pretty for myself at Christmas." She insisted that she was not dating Jimmy then " 'cause he had many girlfriends and had given some of them babies. I wasn't even interested in boys that much at the time." She thought that Jimmy gave her money out of the goodness of his heart and also because of her acquaintance with his sister. (Jimmy's sister had moved to a house on Akosua's block, and Akosua occasionally babysat for her.) Thus it was in Jimmy's sister's house that the future couple saw much of each other. However, Akosua insisted that most of the time Jimmy was in the company of one of his many girlfriends.

Jimmy got out of prison at a critical period in Akosua's life. She was in the process of becoming a regular drug user, and she credited Jimmy with disrupting the process. When Jimmy came out of the penitentiary, Akosua had just dropped out of school. "I had been arrested and was asked to pay a fine of $75. I couldn't take it any more. . . . Aunt Terry? She didn't care about me any more; the only thing she cared about was the reefer I brought her or the money I gave her." Neighbors were beginning to whisper that Akosua had become a "crackhead," but she denied that the name calling bothered her. "It didn't bother me," she said, " 'cause I knew that some of them were crackheads themselves and would sooner or later end up going to rehabs, but I didn't." Before Akosua got too far with street life, she met Jimmy again. Akosua described her meeting with Jimmy as follows:

> See, when I started out I was never a person who wanted to run
> the streets. . . . If it [i.e., the reunion with Jimmy] had been three

or four months later I'd be lost to the streets 'cause I began to
lose weight and I was looking terrible and feeling miserable. My
hair began to fall out and everything seemed to fall apart. I
couldn't take it any more.

Jimmy's marriage proposal rescued young Akosua from what looked
like a slippery road ahead.

REGINA: AKOSUA'S CONFIDANTE

After almost two years of marriage, Jimmy has remained an important
influence in his wife's life. However, he is not the most "significant
adult" in Akosua's life. That distinction goes to her childhood friend
and confidante, Regina, the shadowy figure Akosua describes as "my
best friend in the whole world." The only person Akosua listens to seriously is Regina. Akosua loves and cares for Jimmy, but as she once
confided to me, "I no longer listen to him as I did when he just came
out of prison. Now I am my own woman, and I have two children to
take care of. . . . Regina is like an older sister to me. We get along
'cause we respect each other." That Akosua lived in a homeless shelter on South Second Avenue and had no access to a private telephone
did not disrupt her daily contact with Regina.

Regina was 28 years old and had been legally blind since childhood. Regina was able to do things around the house as though her
eyesight was not severely restricted. In addition, she was gifted with a
beautiful voice and once came in second during amateurs' night at the
famous Black Entertainment Theater in Central City. Although Regina was almost a decade older than Akosua, they related to each
other as peers.

Akosua says that her first "joint" (marijuana) was shared with Regina when she was about 11 or 12 years old (the joint had been stolen
from Aunt Terry's room, but she did not even realize it was missing).
As Akosua explained, "Me and Regina are very tight 'cause we were
home together all the time. She don't go out and I don't like going out
that much. I'm kind of a homey type of person." She described Regina
as "the most beautiful person I ever met. . . . People say she is another
Aretha Franklin and that kinda of stuff; that's true, but for me it's her
total personality and her humanity."

Besides being a wonderful human being and a highly talented singer, Regina was also an ambitious entrepreneur who operated an efficient enterprise in the underground economy. For example, she sold stolen goods brought in from Virginia by her relatives. She had also engaged in activities that she later said she was "not proud of, but . . . when you live here in the ghetto, you learn to survive and take care of yourself." At first she was reluctant to elaborate on this; later on I learned that Regina worked as an "invisible" manager for her cousins who sold drugs in Central City. She had recruited a crew of girls she relied on, including Akosua, and they would assemble in her house to package "nickel" and "dime" bags of marijuana and vials of crack for sale on the streets. Her cousins who lived in an inner-city neighborhood in Central City supplied the drugs in bulk, and after packaging them in Southland, Regina returned them to her cousins to sell in Central City.

In Southland, mostly women did the packaging of illegal drugs discreetly at home. This occurred because the young men who once did this kind of work were already in jail, prison, or on probation/parole; others might be under surveillance by the Narcotics Task Force of the Fayerville Police. As a result, drug dealers chose to contract women who were less of a security risk than young men. It was not a regular occupation, and the women were not employed directly by drug dealers who lived in Fayerville; rather, a contact person like Regina hired them. The work was a temporary operation that was shifted from one apartment or house to another to minimize the chances of detection by the police and cut down on losses from confiscation.

Although Akosua worked for Regina, their friendship was not dependent on their involvement with illegal drugs. They were friends long before Regina's cousins began to involve her in their drug operation. When the two women got together, they did not always talk about drugs; their topics of conversation ran the gamut of their lives. They talked about the necessities of life, current events, the behavior of persons they both knew, happenings in their own lives, events in the neighborhood, and music. They also talked a lot about money, Akosua's two children, and Jimmy's excessive drinking.

Regina was more than the godmother of Akosua's children. She was really their other mother. Aunt Terry said that Akosua's relatives back home in North Carolina complained about her attachment to that "blind woman," which had allowed her a modicum of independence from her immediate family. Akosua responded that she was not worried because "some friends are better than your own kind [relatives].'' Thus in Akosua's eyes, her relationship with Regina was certainly better than that with any of her own relatives.

That Regina, the most significant adult in Akosua's life, was involved with illegal drugs was a strong influence on Akosua. Although Akosua did not have many friends, she was popular with her peers. She enjoyed her role as a mother and preferred to stay at home with her little children or visit Regina while Jimmy was at work (when he could find a job). When alone, Akosua liked to read novels she borrowed from the Fayerville Public Library. One of her favorite writers was Donald Goines, whose books deal with intrigues and human tragedies in the inner cities. Not surprisingly, a common theme in Goines's books is drug abuse and drug dealing.

LIFE IN THE HOMELESS SHELTER

When I first met Akosua she was pregnant and living in a homeless shelter with her husband and their first son. They occupied a single room at the former Washington Plaza Hotel, which had been renovated and renamed Washington Plaza Family Center. It was a 34-unit shelter, one of two major homeless shelters in Southland. Their room was fairly large (18 by 24 ft.) but sparsely furnished. It contained two large beds with side tables, a love seat, an old color television, and a "boom box" (the only furnishing belonging to the occupants). There was a bathroom with both a bathtub and shower. There was no kitchen, which deprived Akosua, who liked to cook, of the opportunity to prepare her own meals. Residents were not allowed to receive visitors in their rooms and had to let counselors inside whenever they requested. Residents complained that the one daily meal served in the community dining room was tasteless, but management consistently refused their requests to allow them to cook their own meals. As a result, many of them went to soup kitchens at various local churches where they could eat free meals and help prepare them. Because of the lack of cooking facilities, Akosua spent a lot of time in the homes of Regina and Aunt Terry. Jimmy did not like going to either of these places, so the family rarely had meals together except when they ate at the Washington Plaza Family Center.

When Akosua was not at Regina's house or at home with Aunt Terry, she often spent her time with neighbors in the shelter. Since most of the people she knew there were acquaintances, rather than good friends, she did not visit them regularly, or vice versa. Also, she refused to share a joint with anyone who was not her friend. This meant that she shared drugs with only a small group of people. Regina and Akosua would not smoke reefer in the presence of other people they both knew or in public. Akosua repeatedly would say that she did not believe in "foolishness," that is, using drugs defiantly in public.

Once, while walking through a narrow, dimly lit alleyway near the Washington Plaza shelter, Akosua and I saw two shelter residents smoking crack. They excitedly exchanged greetings with Akosua, their excitement being the apparent effect of the crack they were smoking. They offered Akosua the pipe to take a few draws and she thanked them, but declined the offer. Whereupon one of the women said: "I thought you are my friend, what's the matter with you acting as if you are different?" Akosua responded, "I'm no different, it's just that I don't feel like it." "Oh, yeah?" replied the woman, who appeared to be insulted by Akosua's behavior. She went on, "When have you smoked [with us]? You always just say no. What's the matter with you? Can't trust nobody, huh? Honey, let me tell you somethin'; you can't live in this world like that. . . ." Akosua snapped at her, saying that she was working as my research assistant. Condescendingly, she told them, "You all don't understand that I don't go for that [implying smoking or drinking on the job], don't you? Now cut it out!" The two women appeared satisfied with her explanation as she turned to me and said: "Let's go Kojo." As Akosua and I walked away, the women could be heard jokingly threatening to tell Akosua's husband about seeing her alone with a stranger at night. When they got out of earshot, Akosua explained to me that they were being difficult because they knew she did not trust them, despite her reference to one of them as a friend some time ago.

Because most of the residents at the Plaza had drug and alcohol problems, there were stringent rules forbidding the use or sale of drugs or alcohol on the premises. However, Akosua managed to sell marijuana, cocaine, and crack clandestinely to some of the residents who, although they were in treatment programs, continued to use drugs or alcohol. While other residents had been caught with drugs and expelled, Akosua had successfully eluded detection for almost two years. Other shelter residents suggested that part of the reason for this was Akosua's charming personality as well as her nonthreatening public persona. But more important was that she did not bring drugs into the building; instead she made her transactions outside. Her secret, she said was: "You must use your head and don't get too greedy." Although she confirmed that her husband did not want her selling drugs, her attitude was: "Jimmy saved me from the streets, and I fell in love with him for that and married him. . . . But that gives him no right to get into my business." Why not? " 'Cause he's my husband not my father."

Akosua was popular among the female residents in this shelter; they came to her with their problems, and she functioned as a de facto counselor. They trusted her because she did not discuss other people's problems in public. She rarely engaged in gossip or trash talk about her fellow shelter residents except with her confidante, Regina.

Akosua's primary responsibility centered on taking care of her two little boys. Unlike many of her neighbors, the day began early; she was up by seven o'clock. First she bathed the boys and gave them cereal for breakfast, then she cleaned their one-room apartment before taking PJ to the childcare center (Shawn was too young, so she kept him with her). She attended a life skills program in the mornings, such as classes in parenting, drug abuse awareness, and preparing for the GED. The Washington Plaza Family Center social workers arranged these programs, which residents were required to attend. In the afternoons, Akosua was able to attend to personal chores, such as visiting the doctor or going shopping. Because there was little privacy in the Plaza, most residents—including Akosua—spent a lot of time outside the premises, in the homes of friends or relatives (fictive kin). As mentioned previously, when Akosua was not in the shelter, usually she was at either Regina's or Aunt Terry's, where she took her children on the days she attended classes at College Opportunities, Inc.

Many of Akosua's peers attributed their drug use to the lack of local entertainment or sporting facilities in the neighborhood. A common statement I heard among the social service/drug treatment providers in the Southland was: "When you have nothing else to do to entertain yourself, what do you do?" But unlike most of her peers, Akosua did not like going out that much.

> Jimmy always wants to take me to the movies [in Yorkville or Rosedale], but I wouldn't go. I prefer to stay at home and watch television or play with my kids instead. . . . When he goes out with his buddies, he doesn't stay long because he would be worrying about what I'm doing at home and return soon. He is uncomfortable about leaving me and my kids alone at night.

Drug Use Behavior

It was difficult for Akosua to abstain from drugs completely. "Every now and then, before I got pregnant again, I used to sneak out and get a little hit 'cause I felt like [I was] missing out on something," she would tell me. Yet she did not consider herself an addict because she could stop for as long as a month or two. She smoked both marijuana and crack, but preferred reefer " 'cause it makes you wanna eat and go to sleep." She smoked reefer at least once or twice a month and cocaine about every other month. She had experimented with angel dust (PCP) but did not like how it made her feel (she described the experience as "losing control" of herself). As a result, she decided to stay away from angel dust, referring to it as a "dangerous" drug. Another drug that Akosua considered as dangerous was heroin. Unlike angel dust, she would not even try heroin because she was afraid of needles and did not want to risk getting HIV.[3]

Akosua hated being labeled a "crackhead" because "it makes you feel like you are from Mars or somethin' like that." According to Akosua, crack got bad press " 'cause we [Blacks] use it. It's all prejudice. Any drug, I don't care what it is, if you use too much of it you gonna get zonked [i.e., lose control of yourself]." Akosua was the first person to convince me that, contrary to news media reports, one can smoke crack intermittently and that crack is not instantly addictive. She did not consider crack to be the most dangerous drug ever to appear on the drug scene in Southland. Like many women in this neighborhood, she believed that alcohol, though legal, was the most destructive drug. By this she meant that alcohol was the most damaging, but not the most dangerous; according to her, the most dangerous drug was angel dust.

Aunt Terry saw no reason why drug addicts or dope dealers should be "hounded like dogs." She had no problem with the young men and women in the projects who used and sold drugs because "they don't bother nobody." She did not perceive drugs—except for crack—to be dangerous in and of themselves. She said she had "known many men, good men, who used dope but did not bother nobody." The ones she could not stand were drunks. "They are in worse shape and need more help than drug addicts," she was convinced. Akosua shared this sentiment. She blamed police crackdowns ("the war on drugs") for the violence and problems associated with drugs in this neighborhood:

Kids in this neighborhood don't have jobs, yet they must take care of their mothers and little sisters. Hauling them to jail or prison is not the answer. It hasn't solved anything. In prison the kids learn how [to] become criminals. They come out and rob, kill people for their money. My husband Jimmy, he doesn't do none of that 'cause he knows I will not tolerate any kind of foolishness like that—robbing old ladies of their social security; that's mean, really sick. If you want to rob somebody, go to the bank, that's where all the money is kept. Don't rob an old lady who is struggling just to stay alive.

Although Akosua claimed to have stopped using drugs when she was pregnant with her second boy, she did not stop selling drugs. She explained that she occasionally sold crack and reefer in order to make ends meet:

I didn't do drugs when I had the baby in my stomach. I had stopped smoking [crack or reefer] because I was scared of the baby coming out messed up. I don't want to bring a crack baby into this world. No baby should be born addicted to crack. I want my baby to be all right. . . . I saw on television pictures of tiny babies with all them tubes and patches; it looked like they couldn't breath. It was scary. . . . [However] when Jimmy got laid off, I'd sneak out and sell reefer or crack 'cause we needed the money.

ECONOMIC SUPPORT

Akosua told me that there was not much money to be made from selling either crack or marijuana in Fayerville in the summer of 1990:

You all think there is a lot of money selling crack. Well, let me tell you somethin'. Selling crack is no prosperity in Fayerville. A vial of crack costs just three dollars in Southland. Here in Fayerville people don't have that kinda money to buy a five-dollar vial they do in the city [Central City].

Nevertheless, Akosua maintained that early in 1990 she sold as much as $300 worth of crack cocaine and marijuana per week. "But," she added, "some of my customers couldn't pay me right away. They had to wait for their [welfare] checks to arrive before they could give me my money."

Akosua had been on welfare practically all her life so she was sympathetic to those on welfare. In the fall of 1990, she received altogether $600 a month from AFDC (i.e., $300 in food stamps and $300 in free rent, because of her two children). Her rent allowance was paid directly to the operators of the Washington Plaza Family Center. Jimmy got about $300 from the social services department, but his eligibility had expired, and he only got the money because of an oversight. Akosua often told me that she would like to get off welfare, but she could not because she had no regular job. Like many welfare recipients, she disliked social workers who controlled her life because she was on welfare. "A lot of things are forced on you," she lamented. "Social services has a lot to do with welfare mothers selling drugs in this neighborhood because they don't give us enough allowance. Receiving welfare checks makes you a client of the social welfare department." She felt that "the real person [self] is seldom seen by the people themselves because we are forced to be something other than ourselves."

Remarkably, Akosua, unlike other welfare recipients in this neighborhood, had no guilt about being on welfare. She did not think less of herself because she was on welfare, nor did she accept the notion that she should be grateful for the public assistance she was receiving. In her eyes, welfare recipients, as well as other poor people who participated in the underground economy, such as drug dealers, were contemptible only if they came to share "the White man's" contempt for them. Whenever the subject of Blacks on welfare was brought up in conversation, Akosua was quick to point out that there were more Whites than Blacks on welfare or that more Whites use illegal drugs than Blacks.

CONCLUSION

Both Akosua's deceased parents as well as her subsequent guardians and significant adults smoked marijuana regularly while she was growing up. Thus it was not unusual that she, too, began to smoke marijuana and later experimented with other illegal drugs. Even after she left home, she established ties with persons who smoked marijuana and used other drugs as well. When her Aunt Terry warned her about the possibility of getting hooked, Akosua scoffed at the idea. She knew too many people, including Granny and Aunt Terry, who smoked reefer for many years. The phrase "getting hooked" has two implicit meanings: (1) becoming socially destroyed by the drug, and

(2) becoming addicted to it. Akosua knew that her aunt's warning was meant to scare her and that marijuana smoking did not do any of those harmful things. Akosua told me that she did not believe in the widespread theory of being hooked on any drug to the extent that one cannot quit even if one were determined to stop. She cited her own intermittent use of crack as evidence.

Akosua's exposure to illegal drugs, perhaps more than that of any of my key informants, indicates the significance of the family/community context. The major elements of this social context such as the community's liberal attitude toward drugs in general or the ambivalent attitude toward marijuana smoking of the adult members in Akosua's household all contributed to the young woman's experiment with marijuana and eventual involvement with all sorts of illegal drugs. If these factors had been taken into consideration in determining the government's policy on drugs, the outcome could have been different. The lack of community or local input into drug policy has left us with a singular drug policy (the so-called law enforcement approach) that seeks to wipe out drug use at all costs.

NOTES

[1] Akosua is the name the Akan peoples of West Africa give to every female child born on Sunday (a male born on Sunday is called Kwasi). My name Kojo, which is an anglicized form of Kwadwo, indicates a male born on Monday. I gave her the name "Akosua," not only because her aunt said she was born on a Sunday, but more important, because her real name is African.

[2] Refers to a male born on Saturday, and the female counterpart is called Amma.

[3] Although heroin can be smoked when sprinkled on marijuana, or it can be snorted, few people in this neighborhood used it in either of these ways; rather, they used heroin intravenously. However, the youths liked to sprinkle their marijuana with cocaine or angel dust and roll it in an emptied-out wrapping called a "blunt."

CHAPTER 5

Dread
The Baccra Maasa

I met Dread in the spring of 1990 with the assistance of his former girl-friend Liz, one of my key informants. Even though Liz and Dread no longer dated, they remained friends. Dread's mother, Colleen, worked as a part-time seamstress for Liz's mother, Sister Sylvia Payne. Their two families were neighbors who lived on the same block where street-level drug sales were rampant in the 1980s and early 1990s. Before we went to meet Dread in his mother's apartment, Liz had cautioned me to be careful when talking with Dread because she thought he had become paranoid as a result of difficulties he was experiencing in reaching his goal of owning his own electronic or automotive business.

Dread was born and raised in Kingston, Jamaica. In 1987, when he was 19, he came to the United States with his older brother, Patrick (who was 22 years old at the time). They came to join their mother, Colleen, who had immigrated to the United States 13 years earlier. Their father had been killed in an automobile accident, so their mother Colleen had left them in the custody of their older sisters, Claudette and Paulette. A few years later the sisters also left Jamaica in search of better economic opportunities in the United States. For all practical purposes, their departure left the two boys to grow up by themselves, although they were put under the supervision of their oldest brother, Winston, who was married and would soon have children of his own.

According to Dread, when he lived in Kingston, he learned "to survive by any means necessary," including the sale of marijuana. The boys' situation was less desperate than Dread made it out to be, however, since there were other kinsmen (aunts, uncles, and older cousins as well as older brothers) around to offer protection and assistance when necessary. In fact, Dread and Patrick were better off than most of their peers because their mother and sisters regularly sent them packages that included money, food, clothing, shoes, and other consumer goods.[1] The money and consumer goods allowed Patrick and Dread to engage in all sorts of illegal activities, including drug use. Patrick provided another explanation for their involvement with marijuana and cocaine. He explained that most of the adult males in their house, including his oldest brother, Winston, smoked ganja. He said that in the 1980s marijuana smoking was commonplace in his native Kingston, the birthplace of the Rastafarian movement. Cocaine too had become increasingly available in Kingston as traffickers used the island of Jamaica for transshipping cocaine between South America and the United States. Furthermore, Patrick maintained, "We always had plenty of food to eat and a little extra money in our pockets," facilitating their involvement with illegal drugs.

Dread and Patrick's mother, Colleen, told me on different occasions that she felt responsible for her two boys' involvement with illegal drugs. She explained that her neglect—that is, leaving her sons to grow up in Kingston without parental supervision—had led to their dabbling in marijuana smoking, which escalated to include cocaine. Her daughter, Paulette, disagreed, arguing that there was very little her mother could have done to prevent the boys from becoming involved with drugs because "many people did the same thing [leave their children behind in Jamaica]. Marijuana is not as dangerous as Americans say it is," she maintained.

Like most residents in Southland, Colleen did not regard marijuana as a dangerous drug either; she shared the widespread belief among Jamaican immigrants that marijuana or "the herb," as young Jamaicans refer to it, is God's gift to man. What seemed to bother her about her sons' marijuana smoking was that it was illegal, and she was concerned about potential arrest and the possibility of serving time in jail. On one occasion, as the two of us were having a conversation, Colleen said that she would probably smoke marijuana if it were not against the law. She added that she had used fresh marijuana leaves as a tonic to prevent ailments, such as cold and fever, in her native Jamaica. Her husband, Geoffrey, also defended the medicinal benefits of marijuana. However, they both regarded cocaine, heroin, and angel dust as "dangerous" and were strongly opposed to their use, especially crack. Almost all the adult household members, with whom Dread and Patrick interacted regularly in Kingston and later in Fayerville, were opposed to these so-called dangerous drugs even while approving marijuana use. Although Dread said he did not find the adult attitude toward drugs problematic, he admitted that it could easily confuse impressionable adolescents, such as his 12-year-old nephew Troy.

SOCIAL RELATIONSHIPS

When Dread and Patrick arrived in the United States, they settled with their mother and other relatives in a two-bedroom apartment located in the notorious section of Southland known as "Jamaican Alley." (Jamaican Alley is a nickname given by African-American neighbors because of the high concentration of Jamaican and other West Indian immigrants.) This area was saturated with drugs and gained national notoriety in July 1988 when, in front of television cameras, the Drug Enforcement Administration (DEA) confiscated some of the contents of an entire apartment building because it found some tenants to be packaging and selling crack.

When I met Dread, his household consisted of: his mother Colleen; his stepfather, Geoffrey (who moved out two years after he and Patrick arrived from Jamaica); his 12-year-old nephew, Troy; and his five-year-old niece, Tracy, whose mother, Paulette, lived in a nearby borough of Metropolitan Central City. His older brother, Patrick, was in jail at this time; he had been arrested for selling cocaine to an undercover police officer. Dread had other close relatives, such as Mr. Morris and Aunt Chi-Chi, both siblings of his mother, all of whom lived in nearby municipalities. Other extended family members lived in other states and therefore had less regular contact with Dread. Besides his brother Patrick, two of Dread's cousins were also serving long prison sentences for drug-related crimes.

Although Dread's network of friends mostly consisted of Jamaican young adults, he also interacted regularly with many adults, mainly West Indians. The only African-American male he interacted with on a fairly regular basis was Mr. Payne, the father of his former girlfriend, Liz. Mr. Payne was married to a West Indian woman. The Payne family was very actively involved with a Pentecostal church. They had hoped to recruit Dread, but they gave up their efforts once Liz told them that they were wasting their time. Another significant adult for Dread was a 47-year-old Jamaican named Carlton, who was the owner of a two-family house down the block. Carlton's wife, Daphne, and Dread's oldest sister, Claudette, had attended the same elementary school in Jamaica. Dread sometimes borrowed money from either Carlton or his wife. Carlton did not encourage or condemn anyone smoking marijuana, but he warned against cocaine, especially its smokeable form (crack), which he had nicknamed "the destroyer." But even his warnings were lukewarm, inconsistent, and often came in the context of laughter, so that neither Dread nor any of his friends took them seriously. Dread spent time in Carlton and Daphne's home, but not as much time as Colleen thought. Colleen was suspicious that perhaps Carlton was the supplier of the cocaine to her sons.

Dread and about a dozen or so Jamaican friends, who lived in Jamaican Alley, called themselves the Jamaican Crew. However, the Southland community knew them as the Jamaican Posse or the Untouchable Posse. Older Jamaican immigrants said that the Untouchable Posse is the name of a notorious gang back home in Jamaica. African-American neighbors say that the name originates from the widely held rumor that they were an organized Jamaican criminal gang whose activities included marijuana and cocaine distribution. Yet, despite this reputation, the police rarely arrested any of the members. It was also rumored that some members of the Jamaican Crew might be police informers. The source of this particular rumor was a rival gang, known as the Lynch Mob, made up of mostly African-American youths who had been arrested and/or incarcerated for a variety of offenses. This rumor added to the tension that already existed between these two rival youth groups or crews.

Dread rejected the assumption that he and his friends constituted a gang, in the traditional sense of a criminally organized, voluntary association. Instead, he described his group as "partners." He said that partners are neighborhood young men whose sole purpose is "to defend ourselves and protect our women from assaults [as well as insults] by others [African-American young men] who have no respect for themselves." The Jamaican/Untouchable Posse then seems to be a crew of immigrant youths whose behavior projects an image similar to a gang.

The rivalry between the Jamaican Crew and the Lynch Mob reflects a deeper ethnic problem in the Black community of Fayerville. Some African Americans complained privately that the local police treated Jamaicans differently from themselves. The fact that the first Black Mayor of Fayerville was a Jamaican immigrant tended to give credence to this complaint. Indeed, it did appear as if Jamaicans were harassed less and received greater leniency when apprehended. However, this may be due in part to the fact that Jamaican parents generally did not hesitate to reprimand their youngsters in front of police officers. As a result of such actions, the officers perceived the majority of the Jamaican youths to be "okay," especially those who had not been here too long, or those who had not lost their accent, or those who had not assimilated American attitudes and behavior. Perhaps of greater significance was that the Fayerville police believed that Jamaican youths dealt only marijuana, considered a soft drug in this community. Although the police arrested young people caught selling marijuana, their prime targets appeared to those involved in the distribution of hard drugs, such as cocaine, crack, heroin, or angel dust. However, if an officer thought that a teenager had an "attitude problem," the youth was arrested immediately, regardless of his or her ethnicity.

I asked Dread why he had never been arrested, while his older brother Patrick, not a member of the posse, had been arrested twice. At first he appeared reluctant to respond, saying that he did not know, but later he attributed his brother's arrest to stupidity:

> Acting stupid, man. That's what got him into trouble. . . . No Jamaican gets arrested selling drugs in Fayerville [i.e., Southland]. You look it up [in the newspaper] and tell me how many Jamaicans you find arrested for selling drugs? Them [the police] arrest us for something else. Me no say it can't happen [lead to a drug charge later]. . . . That's what happened to Patrick. Once they caught him [for disorderly conduct], them became suspicious and kept an eye on him until he was busted for drugs. He became a target. Me telling you, man, once you become a target, forget it, they'll come and get you whenever they need a body to arrest. . . . But few Jamaicans here get caught up with drugs [implying arrested for drugs].

Dread's statement could be challenged on the grounds that three of his own relatives were in prison for drug-related crimes. However, the statement also implicitly raises the issue of different treatment by the police toward young people from different ethnic backgrounds. In the Southland community there was the perception that due to Jamaican youths' tendency to cooperate with the police when arrested, they received special treatment by police. Some members of the Jamaican Posse were in fact reputed to be police informers, although Dread vehemently denied it.

Even though Patrick was not a member of the Jamaican Posse, he knew all the members and was on friendly terms with them. Yet when he was incarcerated, none of them, including his brother Dread, visited him in jail. Once, when Colleen asked Dread to drive her to the jail about 15 miles away from Fayerville to visit his older brother, Dread called and asked me to take her because he was busy conducting interviews for this study. Later he admitted that, as a matter of principle, he did not want to visit jails or prisons. He added that he knew other inmates there besides his brother who had been unjustifiably arrested and incarcerated. He also mentioned his opposition to a body search (all visitors had to go through this process), which kept him away from public places like jails and prisons. He kept in touch with Patrick through messages given to Patrick's girlfriend.

Patrick's incarceration did not seem to make much of an impression on Dread, who said that the threat of incarceration would not influence his decision to continue selling illegal drugs. He did not want to be arrested but, as he put it, "if it happens, it happens. Me kaan't be worried about something like that." Dread's reputation as a risk-taker is reflected in this statement as well as in his desire to try his hands at something new as long as it could fetch him money.

Pattern of Drug Use/Sale

Dread primarily sold marijuana and cocaine powder (cocaine hydrochloride). He sometimes sent Troy to deliver the drugs to customers who lived in Southland. One day I was in the secondhand clothing and furniture store, where my storefront office was located, with Mrs. Sylvia Payne when Troy came to borrow her bicycle. Mrs. Payne later told me that she suspected that the 12-year-old boy was going to use the bicycle to deliver drugs on behalf of his "big brother," actually Uncle Dread. Although she claimed to be an opponent of illegal drugs, Mrs. Payne did not ask or confront Troy about his purpose in borrowing the bike. Instead, she warned him not to give the bicycle to any of his friends; otherwise, she would charge him for it. Troy promised not to give the bicycle to anyone and to return it as soon as possible. Mrs. Payne did not mention this episode to Troy's grandmother, Colleen.

On a few occasions I observed Dread exchanging crack vials for money, but he always denied selling crack, which he demonized as the "devil's drug." On the other hand, he spoke of marijuana as God's gift to "man" (human beings), referring to it as the "herb" mentioned in the Bible as growing on King Solomon's tomb. Patrick introduced Dread to marijuana smoking in Jamaica and to cocaine sniffing in the United States. However, Dread maintained that Patrick's role in both instances was to serve as a conduit to the supplier until he developed his own contacts and reliable sources of supply. When I met Dread, he smoked marijuana regularly—at least five times a day (morning, late morning, afternoon, evening, and night)—and snorted cocaine sparingly, mostly at parties with friends. He would not identify his source of supply, insisting that, for the purpose of protection, his suppliers should remain anonymous. Even though I did not meet his suppliers, it was common knowledge that they were other West Indians in Central City who got the drugs from Ft. Lauderdale or Miami, Florida. When it came to alcoholic beverages, Dread preferred drinking imported Red Stripe beer or stout from his native Jamaica; surprisingly, he did not like rum, a staple drink of Jamaica and the Caribbean in general.

Dread believed that cocaine in the form of crack was Satan's poison designed to destroy the mind of the Black man. When I asked him why he still used cocaine, he responded that he did not smoke crack at all and only rarely sniffed cocaine powder. He admitted to having experimented with crack out of curiosity, but decided against it because it could "mess up" your mind. According to Dread, he got into selling cocaine because the neighborhood was saturated with people selling marijuana. "Nobody can make money selling ganja alone; there are too many [small-time] hustlers out here selling—it's like everybody is over everybody else." At one time it seemed like every teenage boy over 12 years old on his block sold marijuana or cocaine or crack. Most of the youngsters, according to Dread, sold drugs to earn pocket money that they could not get from their parents.

Dread was not a Rastafarian, but he was sympathetic to their cause of "cultural emancipation," including religious, economic, and political freedoms from Western civilization. He often quoted passages from the Bible, as many Rastas do, that seemingly criticized the "wickedness" of capitalism and lack of social justice for the Black man

(African) in the Western Hemisphere (Babylon). He preferred *ital* foods, that is, mostly vegetarian dishes. He espoused ideas he learned from his stepfather, Geoffrey, who liked to pontificate about what was wrong with the world and how the Black man had to rise up and save himself and the world from certain Armageddon.

When Dread arrived in the United States, he attended Fayerville High School, but he did not even last a year. What was Dread's occupation after he dropped out of school and had no regular employment besides occasionally selling drugs? This is an important question because many young men in Southland found themselves in a similar situation. The answer to this question is, however, not as straightforward as you may think. On the one hand he had become an independent drug peddler like many of his cohorts in Southland. On the other hand, labeling him a "drug dealer" is perhaps inappropriate. He did not sell drugs all the time, nor did he consider himself to be a drug dealer. Also, neighbors did not perceive him as such. To call him a part-time drug dealer would also be inaccurate; when he sold marijuana, cocaine, or crack, he did it on a full-time basis. He sold drugs in order to earn money for a specific purpose. For example, when he needed money to buy a car, he sold drugs for about six to eight weeks and made over three thousand dollars, with which he purchased a used Toyota Camry. However, soon after that, he began to borrow money from his mother and friends, including me, to put gas in the car. Sometimes he would sell drugs to pay back the debts he owed, and then he would stop for a while. When his goal was attained, he would stop selling drugs temporarily until another goal surfaced and it became necessary to resume his drug activities. In between selling drugs, he would pursue other interests, such as cutting hair or doing handy work.

EMPLOYMENT OPPORTUNITIES

Both Dread and his older brother Patrick arrived in the United States without high school diplomas, so they immediately enrolled in Fayerville High School. However, Patrick quickly dropped out while Dread, who was placed in the tenth grade, reluctantly went to school everyday. He was unhappy because he felt that he should have been placed in the eleventh grade, if not the twelfth. He was a very good student and his transcript (report card) from Jamaica confirmed this. At the start of his second semester, he complained of boredom—the work was not challenging and he had already studied in Jamaica what was being taught in the tenth grade—so he began to cut school. He would leave home saying he was going to school but did not. His girlfriend and neighbor, Liz, knew this but did not volunteer to tell Dread's parents. Instead, she told her mother who told Dread's mother Colleen, who said she was surprised and very disappointed when her youngest child too dropped out of Fayerville High School like his older brother Patrick. Colleen immediately found money to enroll Dread in a private electronic and technical school in metropolitan Central City. Initially, Dread showed enthusiasm and great promise because he was interested in "fixing things," but he quit after only six months without explanation. He told me that he did not like the attitude of most of the instructors. This infuriated his mother who had borrowed money to pay the relatively expensive tuition.

After dropping out of Fayerville High School and technical school, all in a six- or seven-month period of time, Dread stayed home without making much effort to enter the regular workforce. Dread said he needed time to think over matters. He said that he did not want to work for someone else, and also he found nine-to-five jobs distasteful. He preferred selling drugs sporadically in order to maintain his freedom. Besides selling drugs, he occasionally worked as a barber in a friend's barbershop and gave him 10 percent of his earnings for renting the space. He was very good at cutting hair (he cut my hair several times), but did not feel ready to work as an apprentice, a requirement that had to be fulfilled before he could secure state certification to open his own barbershop.

The only regular employment Dread held since coming to the United States was when he worked as a laborer for his Uncle Morris, a home builder and repair contractor who lived and did most of his business in a borough of Central City. Mr. Morris used to pick Dread and Patrick up every morning at seven, but he gave up because his nephews were never ready, and he sometimes had to wait as long as 30 minutes for them to wake up and get dressed. He also complained that they smoked marijuana in the homes they were repairing and left the windows open for the smoke to dissipate before the homeowners returned from work. According to Mr. Morris, he warned all his employees several times not to leave the windows open, especially in the winter. He did not object to his workers smoking marijuana per se, because he, too, smoked it, albeit discreetly away from the presence of his wife who outspokenly disapproved of this behavior. She felt it was unbecoming of a contractor (implying a person of middle-class status) to engage in that practice. She referred to young men who smoked marijuana as "them rude boys."

According to Liz, Dread only accepted the invitation to work with his uncle because he wanted to make money to save up to buy drugs to deal for more profit. Thus, in her view, after he had acquired sufficient money to buy marijuana and cocaine for retailing in Southland, he began "acting up." Dread gave a different reason for quitting. He said that his uncle was cheating him and that he was not paying him enough money. Colleen sided with her son against her brother. She maintained that Dread was more skilled than his uncle was, and that Mr. Morris had felt embarrassed by this situation. She accused her brother of not wanting to hire her sons in the first place and claimed that she had to plead with him several times before he had agreed to hire them. Mr. Morris terminated Dread (Patrick had quit on his own) and insisted that he was not going to pay him because he did not show up for work. Mr. Morris denied that the firing was due to smoking marijuana on the job, as Aunt Chi-Chi claimed, because he smoked marijuana himself. Thus, it was unclear exactly what precipitated Dread's firing.

Colleen appealed to me to talk to her son to prevent him from becoming a ragamuffin (a ruffian) and "wasting his life." I thought the best way to go about this was to employ him temporarily to interview his friends for my study and also help him to enroll at College Opportunities, Inc. Colleen was concerned that some members of her extended family were spreading rumors that her two boys had become ragamuffins, selling drugs. She was particularly disappointed because Dread had a reputation as a smart boy with potential to go to college and become a professional.

Colleen said that during the family reunion—which I attended—some relatives gossiped about her two boys, and what they said hurt her. She thought that some of the extended family members had talked to me about her sons' drug use. When I denied this, she appeared relieved but still uneasy. Dread attended the reunion for a brief time. Later, when I asked him why he left so early, Dread said that he did not feel comfortable. What annoyed him most was the frown on the faces of some of his relatives when he was in their midst. His severest criticism was for Aunt Chi Chi, who told the others that Mr. Morris had to dismiss Dread because of repeatedly smoking marijuana laced with cocaine. The mention of Dread's use of cocaine was what alarmed everybody, especially his mother.

GEOFFREY AND FAMILY DYNAMICS

Fifty-seven-year-old Geoffrey Lewis was a Jamaican immigrant who had come to the United States during the 1960s. He married Colleen in 1984, three years prior to Patrick and Dread's arrival in Fayerville. The couple provided a remarkable physical contrast; Colleen was a petite woman standing only 5' 1" tall and weighing about 120 pounds, while Geoffrey was a big fellow—about 6' 3" and weighing about 250 pounds. She was dark-skinned and he was light-skinned. Colleen was descended directly from Africa (her father was a Nigerian sailor), and this may have attracted Geoffrey, a divorcé who described himself as a Garveyite, a follower of the Jamaican Pan-African nationalist, Marcus Garvey. In the early part of this century, Garvey tried to organize the return of Black people in the Western Hemisphere to Africa, which he believed was the only place they could have true freedom and dignity as human beings. Politically, Geoffrey was uncompromisingly a Black Nationalist, and he had vowed to relocate to Africa (preferably to the West African nation of Sierra Leone) following his retirement.

Colleen and Geoffrey's relationship was far from ideal. There are several possible reasons for the tension that existed between them. Dread and Patrick's involvement with illegal drugs was a constant dark shadow. Another contributing factor was the overcrowding and congestion in the apartment. Not only was the two-bedroom apartment too small for the expanded family, but it was also cluttered with barrels containing consumer goods waiting to be shipped to Jamaica. Geoffrey complained incessantly about the lack of space for him to entertain visitors in the living room. He wanted to move to a bigger apartment on the Northside of town. He argued that relocation also might help steer the boys away from drugs because the Northside was a better neighborhood with more frequent police patrols. However, Colleen refused to relocate there, saying that they could not afford the higher rent in that neighborhood. (They paid $650 a month for the two-bedroom apartment in the Southland. It would have cost them at least $750 a month to rent a two-bedroom apartment in the Northside.) Also, contributing to Colleen's reluctance to move away from Southland was her concern about leaving friends who lived in Jamaican Alley.

Colleen's unconventional working hours also contributed to the difficulty in maintaining a smooth marital relationship. She worked two jobs: one, 4:00 P.M.–midnight, and the other, 1:00–5:00 A.M. As a result, Geoffrey often found himself saddled with the responsibility of taking care of their two grandchildren (Troy and Tracy) who lived with them. He had to make sure that they did not stay up too late and that they got up on time for school the next morning. While Dread and Patrick were delighted not to have their mother home at night monitoring their whereabouts, Geoffrey grumbled about it. Geoffrey relished his role as head of the household, yet he loathed the responsibility that came with it. His wife described him as "a loving husband but not a good father." She believed that his failure to perform the role of a good father was attributable to his own early childhood experiences at the hands of his adoptive parents, who cut off his schooling at the ninth grade.

When I first met Geoffrey, I realized that something more fundamental than marital or familial problems seemed to be bothering him. Gradually, it became clear to me that he couldn't read or write. His childhood experience had left him functionally illiterate. Colleen had encouraged him to enroll in an adult class, but he felt too ashamed to reveal his intellectual handicap. His functional illiteracy frustrated him immensely because he could not take advantage of most of the opportunities he found in the United States.

Geoffrey acknowledged that the economic situation in early 1990 had deteriorated for young Black males in particular. He talked about chronic unemployment, low wages for those lucky enough to find work, and the rising cost of living. He was most emphatic about changes in attitudes toward work. Comparing his generation of Jamaican immigrants to that of his stepchildren, he said:

> We were more interested in work. We felt we had to work even when work was scarce and wages was low. Only them poor, them truly needy, received home relief [welfare] back then. Children today got everything they want. Parents buy them things all the time. It was not like that during my time. You got something only during Christmas.

Geoffrey did not think that drugs alone were responsible for the changes in Black youths' attitude toward work. He believed that many factors, including drugs and the easy availability of public assistance, have contributed to young people's lack of interest in work. He did not understand why becoming an alcoholic or a drug addict should enable a person to get on welfare.[2] "You have generations of families whose background is dependence on welfare, why is that?" Geoffrey asked rhetorically. He believed that "young people today have no appreciation for anything because it's given to them free." He thought that those who were on welfare did not want to get off and that very few of them were likely to get off it in due course.

Geoffrey's relationship with Patrick and Dread was an important source of marital friction. Geoffrey had problems with Patrick but got along well with Dread. This may be due to the sharp personality differences in the two boys. According to Colleen, Dread was a "manager" while Patrick was a "dreamer" who was always full of ideas. Colleen maintained that Dread was like his biological father, "always doing things, unafraid." He was bold and determined to risk a lot "to get things done fast, fast, fast, and in his way." He was also a good listener and caught on quickly when "you [told] him something." Patrick, on the other hand, would tell his younger brother what he wanted to do and not do it. Because of this their mother was surprised that Patrick was the one "them catch twice for selling [cocaine]." The fact that Patrick had been arrested twice while Dread, a leader of the Jamaican Crew, had never been arrested reflects a fundamental difference in their personalities and temperaments.

Patrick was easy going and made friends easily because, as their mother put it, "he talked too much." Dread, on the other hand, was reserved and tactful, and he did not always show his emotions. Paulette remembered that as children, "little" fights (quarrels) between the two boys often resulted from complaints by Patrick that Dread had stolen his idea. She said that Colleen would praise or thank Dread for fixing something in the house or solving a problem and Patrick would protest that it was his idea or he told Dread how it could be done and he went ahead and did it. Paulette confirmed what Colleen had already told me about Dread, that he was "good with his hands"; he was good at fixing or repairing electronic devices and enjoyed tinkering with machines. He had acquired his mechanical skills simply by watching his stepfather work on the family car.

Dread is what Jamaicans call a *Baccra Maasa*, translated as a manager or the boss, but its appropriate meaning is an entrepreneur. His pattern of selling drugs, as well as his distaste for nine-to-five jobs (i.e., office or clerical work) and a strong desire to pursue only jobs that offered him a lot of freedom in the workplace, supports my view that Dread is a naturally oriented entrepreneur or risk taker.

The difference in personality and in aptitude of the two boys influenced their relationship with Geoffrey. Dread won his good graces while Patrick was always in the doghouse during the two years that Geoffrey lived with them. Geoffrey's dislike of Patrick upset Colleen, who accused her second husband of favoring Dread over Patrick. According to Colleen, Geoffrey made no effort to hide his dislike of Patrick, always saying that he "was up to no good," and he would not amount to anything in life. Patrick was incapable of getting it right as far as Geoffrey was concerned, and this disturbed Colleen a great deal. It created tension all the time in the house and led Colleen to discuss with her younger daughter, Paulette, the possibility of Patrick going to live with her in Central City. Paulette was sympathetic but managed to persuade her mother to keep Patrick in Fayerville because the police in Central City were notorious for brutalizing the young Black men they arrested. Paulette was more concerned about her brother's drug involvement than his problems with their stepfather.

Colleen thought that Geoffrey's lack of concern for Patrick led him to refuse to accompany her to the police precinct when the young man was arrested. Later, when Patrick was transferred to the county jail about 15 miles from Fayerville, Geoffrey consistently refused to drive Colleen there to see her son. Colleen did not understand why her estranged husband could not forgive Patrick, since "everybody makes mistakes." She said that she was hurt because not once did Geoffrey say, "Let's go and see the boy [in county jail]. . . . That's why I go see him [Patrick]." Colleen said that she had forgiven her son because on a visit he had told her: "Mammy, I know what I put you through. . . . When I get out I will put my life together, and you won't have to worry about me as you do now." Colleen told me that this time she felt her son was sincere, and that made her unable to control the tears that welled up in her eyes and began to stream down her face. In a discussion about Patrick's arrest and incarceration, Geoffrey had this to say:

> If a person don't care [about what he does], whether it's your own son
> or friend or your whatever, if him is doing something wrong, you
> should talk to him, [but] that doesn't mean you hate him. That's me
> way years ago and that's me way today. It will always be me ways.

Colleen agreed with her husband, but she thought that Geoffrey had been too harsh and did not give the boys a chance. She often responded to his criticism with the terse statement, "Nobody is perfect," whereupon Geoffrey would turn to her and say, "Didn't I ask you three or four times to talk to the boys? And whenever I asked if you've talked to them, you said 'Not yet.' That's one hell of a way to be a mother." Colleen did not appreciate that particular comment from Geoffrey, which questioned her fitness as a mother, and she did not let it go unchallenged. Often she would remind Geoffrey that the world had changed since they both "come up" in Jamaica and that he had to deal with the new realities of life. She insisted that her boys "aren't the only ones [using and/or selling drugs]; they all [young people in general] are doing drugs." Then one day she brought up the case of Geoffrey's son from a previous marriage, who was in an upstate prison for killing a drug dealer. But then she quickly added, "I don't mean you or me approve of it, but there is little you or me can do because it's the trend and we have to deal with it." It went on like this, with Geoffrey trying to get at Colleen by criticizing her children. Throughout the heated exchanges, Colleen would insist that if she had failed as a parent, Geoffrey was partly to blame.

Initially there had been a desire on both sides (the boys' and Geoffrey's) to make their new kinship alliance work. The young men had not really had a father-figure in their lives since early childhood, and they were looking forward to meeting their mother's new husband, as Patrick confided to me during a visit to see him in the county jail. Geoffrey, Dread, and Patrick used to watch cricket and wrestling matches on cable television, as well as play dominos, all of which were Geoffrey's great passion.[3] Dread too became passionate about these sports and games; both he and Geoffrey were instrumental in having the cable installed in Colleen's apartment so that they could watch these events on television. All of this prompted Colleen to blame her husband for contributing to her boys' "laziness":

> When they first came, [Geoffrey] drank with them all de time. You could not get any of them to do anythin' around here; them always watched wrestlin' [on television] and played dominos and drank together. . . . Why you think such good and hard-working boys change so fast like that? In Kingston [Jamaica] they did everythin' for themselves. They come here one month and them don't want to do nothin', why is that? How come them change so fast?

In her frustration, Colleen told Dread that she regretted bringing them to United States and, in part, she blamed Geoffrey for encouraging her to do so. At first the boys did not want to come to the United States, but she had insisted and ultimately prevailed.

Geoffrey's influence on the boys stems from the fact that he interacted with them on a daily basis during their first couple of years in Fayerville. He was their father, teacher, big brother, partner, role model, interpreter, and cultural broker; he showed them how to adapt to life in Southland, to Fayerville, and to U.S. society in general. They did not always agree with his viewpoint, but they knew where he stood on most issues. Dread, in particular, tended to agree with Geoffrey's perception of the social reality of Blacks in the United States. Geoffrey's rhetoric of Black Nationalism thus found a sympathetic ear in Dread.

But it was precisely Geoffrey's desire to be a father to Patrick and
Dread that worked against peaceful coexistence. The boys had been
independent for such a long time that they could not tolerate parental
control—being told what they could or could not do. These factors
were to conspire against their efforts to create a harmonious domestic
atmosphere in order to please their mother.

Geoffrey became aware of the boys' involvement with drugs soon
after their arrival from Jamaica. He did not take any action, however,
because he thought that they only smoked marijuana (he denied ever
seeing them use cocaine). Later, when a friend told him that his stepsons might be involved with cocaine as well, he immediately informed
their mother. At the same time, though, he advised her not to confront her sons, because he thought moving the family away from Jamaican Alley into a better neighborhood would correct the problem.
Colleen complained that whenever she tried to speak to the boys, she
did not get any support from Geoffrey. He would not say anything,
and on the few occasions that he actually spoke out against drugs, he
appeared to blame only Patrick. Indeed, Geoffrey confirmed to me
that he thought Patrick was a bad influence on Dread.

Geoffrey had other issues with Patrick's and Dread's association
with drugs. He feared being implicated in a drug conspiracy charge.
Following Patrick's arrest, two plain-clothes detectives came to the
apartment to question Geoffrey, suspecting that he might be the brain
behind a conspiracy to distribute narcotics. Geoffrey denied knowing
anything about drugs being dealt from the apartment. This incident
may have frightened Geoffrey and contributed to his decision to move
out. However, he said that he moved out because "a man kaan't live in
a house where him have no authority." His wife, however, didn't believe that: "No man abandons his family because the children are hard
headed. Tell me, Mr. Kojo, if what he is saying makes sense? If the
children won't listen and misbehave [don't want to do anything except
eat and sleep] you straighten them out," she said with obvious irrita-
tion. After he moved out, Geoffrey tried to convince his wife to join
him and leave the apartment to Dread and Patrick. He felt that if the
boys had to assume responsibility for the rent and the utilities they
would become more disciplined, but Colleen disagreed.

Colleen told me that she was deeply hurt when she realized that
Geoffrey wanted her to choose between her marriage to him and her
sons. When she refused to make such a choice, he told her before
moving out of the family's apartment: "You got your children, it can't
be your boys and me in this apartment. Me can't live with lying, rude

boys; they are your blood, so you don't want [to] kick them out. Well, they are all yours. Me outa here." Geoffrey does not deny uttering these words, although he maintains that he wanted to impress upon his wife the seriousness of the situation at that moment.

Geoffrey moved into a one-bedroom apartment in the Northside of town. His move to the Northside may also have had something to do with raising his consciousness: he was aware that Southland was generally considered a working-class or underclass area, while the Northside was viewed as middle class. Geoffrey was very sensitive to racial or social class distinctions. Before he moved out, however, he had already influenced his stepsons' adaptation to life in the United States. Though he denied this influence on the boys, his role cannot be discounted, especially when one analyzes Dread's drug involvement.

COLLEEN'S PREDICAMENT

Geoffrey insisted that he would return to live in the Southland apartment only after the boys moved out. Although Geoffrey had moved into an apartment by himself in Northside, he still visited Colleen in the Southland, especially on weekends. He gave Colleen $100–$150 every two weeks to cook for him, and she would take the food to his new apartment. When Colleen cooked for Geoffrey, she deliberately refused to leave any of the meals for her children; she gave all of the food to her estranged husband. When I asked how she felt as a mother refusing to share food with her son who was not working, Colleen responded this way: "It hurts inside knowing that my son isn't working and probably going hungry." However, she did not want Geoffrey to think that she was feeding the children he had refused to accept with food that he provided.

Colleen threatened to evict Dread, but she agreed that Dread might be confused because she often told him to move out, yet when he didn't she still gave him food to eat on certain occasions. At times, Colleen refused to serve Dread any food because he did not help around the house (e.g., wash his dirty dishes). Asked where she thought her son got the money to buy food, she replied that his friends gave it to him. On a few occasions I gave him money, which he immediately used to buy a Chinese vegetable dish. I asked him why he did not sell drugs all the time to make certain that he always had money, and

Dread explained that business was slow because his regular customers did not have money to pay for the drugs. The only way to make a profit was to sell to strangers, but he was not going to take that chance.

In addition, Colleen relied on Dread for his car. Without Dread's car (which, you recall, he purchased with the money he had earned selling drugs) Colleen would have been forced to give up her part-time job as an office cleaner in Central City. Public transportation was hard to come by during the late-night hours when she needed to be at work, so Dread's car brought great relief to his mother, although it did not stop her from complaining about Dread's involvement with drugs. What it did do, however, was to force her to tone down her criticism, even though she denied such a change in her relationship with Dread.

Once, while cleaning Dread's room, Colleen found about twenty packets of marijuana and a loaded semiautomatic pistol. She sent for me in my storefront office, a block away. She wanted me to unload the gun so that she could throw it away down the garbage chute. After speaking with me, however, she agreed to my suggestion not to throw the gun away, but to wait and talk to Dread about it. I tried to impress upon her the need to talk to her son calmly but firmly, and to insist on an explanation. On previous occasions, when she had found their apartment reeking of marijuana smoke and had tried to talk to Dread, he had refused to respond, and had accused his mother of being hysterical and prejudicial. This time Colleen decided to leave the gun where she found it, but she took the marijuana and hid it in her bedroom. She then warned her grandson, Troy, not to go into Dread's room until she had talked to him. However, sensing impending trouble, the little boy ran and alerted his uncle Dread (who was with friends in a neighbor's apartment).

Dread decided to stay away from home until after his mother had left for work, at which time he returned to collect the pistol and the stash of marijuana. He found the gun, but the marijuana was missing. The next day, when his mother confronted him, he refused to talk. In her frustration Colleen refused to leave him dinner. A week passed before mother and son resumed talking. Colleen insisted that Dread tell her the whereabouts of the gun, but he denied that he ever had a gun in his room; the only thing he admitted to possessing were the packets of marijuana. Colleen then went to her room, brought out the marijuana, and gave it back to him with a stern warning not to smoke it in her apartment. Then she added: "You better be careful before you, too, end up in jail like your brother. I will not come to bail you, boy. You hear me good now!" Without his mother present, Dread explained to me that he was holding the gun for a friend. I repeated what he already must have heard several times, that his mother was very concerned that he might be killed in a shootout.

ATTITUDE TOWARD ILLEGAL DRUGS

A case had appeared in the newspaper about a Jamaican couple arrested for growing marijuana in their backyard (the marijuana was estimated to be worth $70,000). I discussed the case with Colleen and Geoffrey. They both claimed to know the couple and said the marijuana was for personal use because the man's wife suffered from asthma and chronic colds, so she needed the fresh marijuana leaves for tea. Geoffrey accused the Fayerville police of playing politics with the health of a sick Black woman. He said that the police were trying to make the Jamaican couple a scapegoat in order to embarrass Fayerville's Jamaican-born mayor who was facing a stiff challenge in the Democratic primary election.

Geoffrey—like many adults in this neighborhood—was ambivalent about drugs. He had smoked marijuana as a "young man and . . . did not think much about it." He stopped "the minute [he] became aware of what's really happening to the Black man all over the world." However, he still enjoyed "ganja-rum" (rum that has been cured with marijuana) with his friends. Geoffrey believed in the conspiracy theory that drugs "are deliberately being dumped in minority neighborhoods like Southland by the power structure" (Whites) to keep Black people distracted from educating and improving themselves. That is why he was very disappointed that Dread, who had been a good student, decided to drop out of Fayerville High School. Not surprisingly, Geoffrey blamed Patrick for "teaching" younger brother, Dread, the "dangerous" drug of cocaine.

I had an opportunity to speak with some of Dread's extended family members about drugs at a family reunion held during Christmas celebrations. All the adult males admitted to having smoked marijuana before, and a few continued to smoke it occasionally. The female relatives did not smoke but most had used marijuana leaves for tea or tonic in their native Jamaica. They were more concerned about the dangers of smoking crack and, to a lesser extent, snorting cocaine powder. Also, they perceived heroin to be as dangerous a drug as crack, al-

though their fear of using heroin appeared to derive from
unfamiliarity. None of them had ever tried heroin; the women described its effects in the most horrific terms, such as turning a person
into a monster. The men, on the other hand, knew what heroin was but
claimed they did not touch it because "it [was] too strong and could
make you act like a mad man." Fortunately, they were all aware of the
association of injecting heroin with a dirty needle and contracting HIV.

Conclusion

When I began my ethnographic studies in Southland, among the major questions I wanted to investigate were: How was it possible for
Black youths to engage in the use and sale of illegal drugs when their
parents or guardians were supposedly against illegal drugs? Were par-
ents/guardians in cahoots with their children/dependents to use and/or
distribute illegal drugs? Or did they try to prevent them from becoming involved with drugs, but failed in their efforts?

   The portrait of Dread in particular answers these questions as it
starkly illustrates the paradox that exists in the parental attitude toward their children. Geoffrey clearly saw this in the way that his wife
dealt with his two stepsons, but he couldn't articulate it well to her. It
is difficult to determine whether the boys' drug use caused the eventual breakup of their parents' marriage, but their involvement with
drugs certainly caused tension between Geoffrey and Colleen. The arrest and incarceration of Patrick did not help matters. But Dread's
story shows how intricately intertwined a son's or daughter's involvement with drugs can be with spousal difficulties. It also raises the
question: To what extent does children's drug use contribute to the
breakup of their parents' marriage, and to what extent does the
breakup of marriage contribute to Black youths' involvement with illegal drugs? Earlier we encountered a similar situation, but with a
slightly different twist, between Ron and Brenda Marshall as they
tried to deal with Gerald's involvement with drugs. Different conclu-
sions could be drawn from both case studies, but I think that the most
significant is that drug use is not just a problem that ignites in rebel-
lious misbehaving adolescents. Instead it is normalized throughout the
life cycle: it is learned at an early age in the home and is tolerated, if
not facilitated by older family members.

Dread first became aware of the beneficial use as well as potential dangers of drugs from older relatives in his native Jamaica. His drug career began by smoking marijuana in a society that does not view marijuana use to be problematic, although in Jamaica legal restrictions to marijuana smoking are similar to those in the United States. The absence of Dread's mother from Kingston at the time certainly played a part in his ability to purchase marijuana. Thus both the circumstances of the extended family at the time and the cultural context in which Dread began to dabble in marijuana were significant factors. Dread's regular marijuana smoking and occasional sniffing of cocaine in the United States can also be attributed to both the local cultural context and family circumstances in Southland, which were not very much different from that which prevailed in Kingston. In Southland, marijuana was Dread's mainstay, although whenever he needed money quickly, he sold crack because it was more profitable than marijuana. However, Dread did not regularly smoke crack because of the perception of this drug as dangerous. Dread's behavior thus shatters the old myth that all street drug peddlers abuse the drugs they sell.

NOTES

[1] Children in Jamaica who have been left under the supervision of close relatives while waiting for their parents to send for them and who receive provisions in the form of barrel packages from their parents living in the United States were called "barrel pickni," Jamaican patois, which translated literally means a "barrel child."

[2] A drug addict or an alcoholic must be in treatment to qualify to receive Medicaid and then be assessed for welfare benefits. The addiction, which was treated as a disability, became the means by which people could collect welfare payments.

[3] Dominos is a popular table game in the Caribbean, and it has become increasingly popular in Southland, reflecting the strong influence of West Indians in this neighborhood. Recently tournaments have been organized between the various nationalities from the Caribbean. When Dread and his friends played dominos, they smoked marijuana and drank Red Stripe beer, imported from Jamaica. On these occasions, the players passed around the marijuana joint, as well as the beer bottle, from one person to another. When dominos are played in tournaments outside on a park bench during the summer, the players are very alert to watch out for undercover police or police patrol cars, although only rarely is anybody arrested for smoking a joint under such circumstances.

CHAPTER 6

Denise's Family Fault Lines

I met Denise in 1990 when she was six months pregnant and asked her to be part of the ethnographic study I was conducting in Southland, to which she agreed, and we quickly became friends. She was on probation for a drug-related offense and had enrolled in the Step Forward Program at College Opportunities, Inc., which prepared students for the GED. Officially, the courts had not ordered her into a drug treatment program. However, at the suggestion of the probation department, she sought counseling at the Renaissance Drug Treatment Center, a therapeutic community (TC) located in Southland. Denise told me she needed someone like myself who could advise her on academic matters and assist her with my car from time to time.

Even though Denise was six months pregnant and attended drug counseling, she continued to smoke marijuana and, I'm told, occasionally crack. When I asked why she used these drugs, especially in her present condition, her response was: "I love to get high now 'cause it helps me get away from the haunts, hurts, pains, and [humdrum] of everyday life . . . [marijuana] gets me away nice and easy." She denied smoking crack, saying that fear of endangering the fetus had caused her to stop as soon as she found out that she was pregnant. But she added, "I'm still young and I'm gonna straighten out my life as soon as I have my baby. You know God gave me this baby for a reason, to get my life together before it's too late. I'm still young. How old you think I am? I'll be 18 on September 12, [1990]."

On October 10, 1990 Denise gave birth to a baby boy named Curry at the North General Hospital in Metropolitan Central City. She later told me that it was a joyous occasion but a lonely experience because none of her family members or her girlfriends were around. The baby's father, Flaco, was being held in a Central City jail on a drug charge, and neither he nor any of his family members were there either.

SOCIAL RELATIONSHIPS

Seven-year-old Denise arrived in Central City from Kingston, Jamaica, on a snowy day in January 1980. Her working-class mother had sent her to join her middle-class father, who had married another Jamaican woman. At least initially, Denise, her father, Glen, her stepmother, Rosemary, and her two half-sisters, Tanya and Nicole, all lived together compatibly and comfortably in a single household in South Fairfield, a borough of Central City close to Fayerville. A few years later, the family moved into a beautiful, spacious house in an area that is considered a middle-class enclave in the generally low-income Southland neighborhood.

Glen and Rosemary were both college-educated and had professional jobs with good combined incomes, reportedly over $100,000 a year. Glen worked for a major computer company in a middle-level management position, while Rosemary was a registered nurse at a teaching hospital in Metropolitan Central City. Both Denise and Nicole attended public schools in Fayerville, and their older sister, Tanya, attended an expensive private college in a nearby village. The family's relocation to Southland brought Denise closer to collateral relatives living there. Her close relationship with these relatives and her intense interactions with other Jamaican women, as well as the constant quarrels with her stepmother, would influence her to become involved with illegal drugs.

No other member of Denise's father's household was known to use or sell illegal drugs. Denise told me that her natural mother, Comfort, and her uncles in Jamaica used marijuana regularly. However, as far as I could determine alcohol was the only drug tolerated in Glen's house and was consumed by the adults only on special occasions. Rosemary, the acknowledged head of this household, was concerned about anything her family members did that might tarnish the image she and Glen had carefully cultivated among the Jamaicans in this community. Glen was the former president of the Caribbean Islands Association, an association of West Indian immigrants in Fayerville. He was highly respected in the West Indian Community; at the same time, he tried to keep his three daughters away from many West Indian families, especially those known to have "rude boys" in their midst.

Rosemary was wary of the kind of West Indians with whom Denise had begun to associate. She complained that she had tried to teach Denise how to behave "like a lady," that is, interact selectively with West Indians, without appearing snobbish or arrogant, but that her stepdaughter had reacted with "bizarre accusatory outbursts." Indeed, Denise harshly criticized her stepmother: "She acts sophisticated. . . . They [her parents] had nothin' when they came here. Now they are rich; they think they got everythin' and act as if they always had it." The maneuvering of social relationships by her parents seemed to confuse young, gregarious Denise, who liked to associate freely with people.

Rosemary did not refer to Denise as her stepdaughter; she referred to her simply as her daughter. However, as they began to have bitter disagreements, Denise categorically rejected references to Rosemary as her mother. When asked about this, she insisted: "She is not my mother, she is just married to my father." Their disagreements worsened when Denise refused to sever her relationship with a particular group of Jamaican girls about whom Rosemary had warned her, and she generally began to show insubordination toward her stepmother. At that point Rosemary advised her husband to send Denise away to live with his mother. Glen's mother reluctantly allowed Denise to live with her. So, almost eight years after arriving in the United States from Jamaica, Denise moved out of her father's house and went to live with her grandmother in a different section of Southland. There she began to experiment with marijuana and other drugs and embarked on a lifestyle that would eventually get her in trouble with the law.

MOVING IN WITH OTHER RELATIVES

Denise's new household consisted of her grandmother, Osetta, and her companion, Mr. Thompson, who worked in maintenance for the Fayerville Housing Authority. Osetta and Mr. Thompson lived in a two-family house in a section of Southland considered a high-crime area by the Fayerville police, although it contained working-class households whose members were largely law-abiding. Also living in the house was Denise's uncle, Charles, the younger brother of her father, who was an engineer with the Central City Transit Authority. Renters occupied the apartments on the second floor and in the basement. The tenant on the second floor was a single parent with three young children and who worked part-time as a nurse's aide at Fayerville Hospital. The other tenant in the basement was rarely home because she worked as a live-in maid in a neighboring state. As a precaution against burglary, this tenant left the key to her apartment with Charles. A year after Denise moved to her grandmother's house, her Aunt Cherry joined them, having lost her job and her home due to foreclosure; she came with her 10-year-old son, Dave. Thus Grandmother Osetta's house was crowded. Yet, Denise said she preferred it to her parents' home.

Another important family member was Denise's 82-year-old great-grandmother (Osetta's mother), who had only recently moved into a nursing home in the Northside of Fayerville. She was respectfully called Mrs. Beckford, although she was never legally married. Living in a nursing home had not decreased her influence over the household she once headed. According to Grandmother Osetta, Mrs. Beckford staunchly defended the right of her great-granddaughter to live her life as she pleased. She was instrumental in persuading Grandmother Osetta to allow Denise to come and live in their home; the octogenarian even issued instructions that the room she used to occupy was to be given to her 15-year-old great granddaughter.

Why did Grandmother Osetta hesitate to take Denise into her home, when she was in the habit of complaining to her son, Glen, that, even though he and his family had moved from Central City to Fayerville, she still did not see her grandchildren often? She had even suggested to him once that if he and his wife were too busy to bring her grandchildren over, they should send them in a taxi, and she would pay the fare. Grandmother Osetta explained to me that she was initially reluctant to have Denise live with her because she felt Denise needed supervision, which she could not provide. She expressed this in a rather poignant manner: "Denise is growing up fast, but she isn't becoming an adult." Denise, on the other hand, had her own perception of adults. In a conversation about her relationship with adult relatives, she said:

> Adults are crazy. Them can't make up dem minds. They are confusing. The moment them tell you don't do that or do this . . . they'll tell you to do this 'n then they go, "don't do that. Why did you do that?" It's crazy! Them can't make up them minds. . . . Me and my girlfriends, we don't like adults 'cause they are bossy. . . . I'll be a nice adult, yap! 'cause I'm fun. I don't like adults 'cause they buy you ugly clothes. . . .

Grandmother Osetta felt unable to provide the proper supervision for Denise because she (Grandmother Osetta) led a very active and full life. She was employed as a nurse's aide in the same nursing home where her mother lived, and she participated regularly in activities for seniors as well as in the local Democratic party. She was also concerned that neither Mr. Thompson nor Charles would discipline the 15-year-old Denise, should it become necessary in her absence. Grandmother Osetta was even concerned that Charles would seduce Denise's girlfriends who came to the house. Aunt Cherry, who could provide parental authority or guidance over Denise was, at that time, living with her son in her own house in a different community.

With the exception of Grandmother Osetta, all the adults in Denise's new home smoked marijuana and/or drank alcohol regularly; Uncle Charles snorted cocaine on weekends. Mr. Thompson said that he had given up smoking marijuana but he still drank ganja-rum tonic on weekends. Despite this, Grandmother Osetta denied being aware of any drug use in her house. Her tacit tolerance of illegal drug use in her home was a source of tension between her and Rosemary, and it might have indirectly contributed to the breakup in the relationship between Denise and her stepmother. According to Denise, this rupture occurred when she and Nicole were driving home with their parents after a visit to their grandmother's house. Rosemary began to speak critically about her mother-in-law's failure to order Charles and the other tenants not to smoke marijuana in her house. According to Denise, "It started as a joke or something like that," but the innocuous comment gradually developed into a heated argument between Rosemary and Glen, which continued over the next couple of days. The outcome was that Rosemary swore never to visit Grandmother Osetta's house with the children again until Glen persuaded her to take decisive action (to put an end to the marijuana smoking by her tenants).

Even though Rosemary complained about Charles smoking marijuana in her mother-in-law's house, she was amicable toward her brother-in-law, and when Charles visited Rosemary and Glen's house, she did not raise the issue with him. Unfortunately, Rosemary's contradictory behavior (which was evident to Denise) occurred at a time when Denise was beginning to question and rebel against her stepmother's authority. She began to accuse her stepmother of being a "backstabber" or a "two-sided cutlass." It was the name-calling that prompted Glen to send Denise immediately to live with her grandmother in an attempt to prevent a further rift between his wife and his daughter.

PROBLEMS AT SCHOOL

While living in her grandmother's house, Denise had the freedom to become acquainted with all sorts of people, but she mostly befriended other Jamaican girls. Some of these girls, like her close friend Michelle, did very well in school and went to college after high school; others dropped out of high school. Denise fell into that category of students who might have done well if motivated, but she found classes boring and floundered about until she was dismissed.

When I asked about leaving school prematurely, Denise and her friends gave a variety of answers to explain problems that West Indian students faced at Fayerville High School. The most common one they mentioned was being ridiculed in the classroom because of their Jamaican or West Indian accents. Even Denise's friends who excelled in school mentioned this as a difficult challenge they had to face during their high school careers in Fayerville.

Denise was better able to overcome this handicap than most of the West Indian students I interviewed. Rosemary recognized this early on as a potential dilemma for Denise and took steps to assist her stepdaughter (even before beginning school in Central City) to lessen her Jamaican accent. Denise observed that since she had been in the United States for quite some time, she had learned to minimize her Jamaican accent when it was appropriate (e.g., in communication with non-Jamaicans). Most of the time, however, she chose not to do so, because she was more comfortable speaking English in her native Jamaican dialect. According to Rosemary, Denise stopped making the effort when they moved to Fayerville and she started to associate with a group of Jamaican girls. This situation added to Denise's estrangement from her stepmother.

"Womanish Girls"

"Womanish girls" is a Jamaican phrase that, in this context, refers to Denise's girlfriends who acted older than they were. When I first met Denise, she had many girlfriends, about two dozen or more. Her effective network of associates and girlfriends ranged in age from 15 to 36. Not all of them, however, were Jamaican. She loved people and made friends easily, though she did not make a clear distinction between friends and acquaintances.

Most of the time Denise associated with a core group of about six girls, all of whom were Jamaican. They included Michelle (17), Daphne (18), Donna (18), Precious (19), Josephine (16), and Paulette (17). This list of close friends could be extended to include Darlene (17) and Paula (20), and the so-called "Jamericans," that is, Jamaicans born in the United States. With the exception of Michelle, Rosemary did not want her stepdaughter to associate with any of the other girls because she said they were *stregge,* which means vulgar, uncouth street girls, who came from "disreputable" homes. Denise did not disagree with the characterization of her girlfriends as stregge, but she strongly objected to Rosemary's attempt to deny her the right to choose her own friends. What Rosemary perhaps was not aware of was that all these girls, including Michelle, smoked marijuana, which they called "doobie." Rosemary's concern proved to be well founded. With the exception of Michelle, none of the girls, including Denise, completed high school, and they all gave birth while they were in their teens.

Denise's friendship with these girls introduced her to street life, Afro-Jamaican style, which involves the superimposition of Jamaican symbols and/or Rastafarian ideas on what is essentially an American ghetto lifestyle. These Jamaican youths dressed in fanciful clothes with bright red, yellow, green, and black colors; they wore Travel Fox sneakers; the females wore fat dookie earrings. Their male counter-parts displayed the Jamaican flag inside their cars; they used and sold illegal drugs, mostly marijuana, which they also called ganja or the herb. They patronized Jamaican restaurants and frequented night-clubs that specialized in West Indian and African music.

The nonstop partying, the hanging out on the streets until late at night, and the peddling and use of drugs all began to distract Denise from her academic work, and she started to cut classes. Her school sent letters to her parents, but since they were mailed to her grand-mother's address, Denise was able to intercept them. Eventually, she was expelled from school during the eleventh grade. Her expulsion caused a change in her relations with her family. Her father immedi-ately discontinued her allowance and appealed to other household members not to give Denise money. Only Grandmother Osetta com-plied; the rest, especially her great grandmother, Mrs. Beckford, dis-regarded Glen's request and gave Denise money when she could afford it, thus preventing Glen's financial squeeze from having the in-tended impact on Denise's behavior.

Denise's dismissal from school cost her something more impor-tant than money, however: the parental support she had received from the mother of Michelle, one of her closest Jamaican girlfriends, soon stopped. Michelle's mother had treated Denise as if she were her own daughter, but now she put restrictions on access to her home, forcing the two girls to drift apart. The 36-year-old mother told me that she was less concerned about her daughter smoking a "little marijuana joint once a while" than dropping out of school. Michelle's mother would no longer permit Denise to sleep at Michelle's house. Michelle concealed her visits to Denise's home, which was not too far away from her own.

Neighbors who knew the two girls had different opinions about the action Michelle's mother took and its subsequent effect on Denise. Some argued that had Michelle's mother not tried to end her daugh-ter's friendship with Denise, Denise might not have gotten into trou-ble with the law or become pregnant. Others were more sympathetic to Michelle's mother, saying that Denise was stubborn and always did what she wanted so she would have gotten into trouble anyway.

Upon her dismissal from school Denise moved out of her grand-mother's house. She lived with older Jamaican women whose little children she babysat from time to time. Because these women sold and used drugs, Denise's own drug use became more regular than before.

Pattern of Drug Involvement

According to Denise, her desire to experiment with marijuana first surfaced when she visited her grandmother's house and watched Uncle Charles share a joint with the woman who lived in the basement. She also heard them talk about the benefits of marijuana smoking. For example, Charles, who brought files from his job to work on at home, said that marijuana helped him to concentrate on his work. The tenant in the basement talked about returning home from scrubbing floors, washing dirty clothes, and cooking for her employer's family to relax with a smoke of marijuana. On other occasions, when Denise found Uncle Charles smoking marijuana with his friends, they talked about the aphrodisiac effects of marijuana smoking. When asked about her memories of people explaining the effects of the drug, she said that she did not remember any of them saying that marijuana got them high. Denise said the term "high" was used by her Uncle Charles to describe his feelings after snorting cocaine. Charles defined the concept of high as a "feeling of ecstasy" and confirmed that he got that sensation only from snorting cocaine.

Denise's actual involvement with illegal drugs began a week or two after she joined her grandmother's household. She saw her Uncle Charles smoking ganja and asked if she could try it. Charles consented because he did not believe that marijuana was addictive or dangerous. Charles insisted, "The so-called experts who say that ganja is addictive and dangerous haven't smoked a joint in their life, [so] how can them be so sure about its effects? I'm telling you, those clinical trials are suspect because there are so many uncontrolled variables . . . . Don't believe what they say, man!" Yet, as soon as his niece began to cough and showed signs of an anxiety attack, he snatched the joint from her and refused to allow her to continue the experiment with smoking marijuana. Denise admitted to being struck by an anxiety at that time, but said that she wanted to continue smoking the joint anyway. She had to wait until a few weeks later, when a girlfriend taught her how to smoke and enjoy marijuana properly. Interestingly, Denise discounted the fiasco with her uncle and claimed, instead, that her first experience smoking marijuana was with her girlfriends.

Michelle, who Rosemary thought was a good role model for Denise, knew how to smoke marijuana before Denise did. Denise explained that she began to smoke marijuana regularly with Michelle in

Denise's house when her grandmother was not home. They usually smoked a spliff or two. They could not smoke in Michelle's house " 'cause Michelle's mother could be a bitch." Often they burned incense in her room to muffle the marijuana odor, but Grandmother Osetta was not easily fooled, and she would cuss, holler, and threaten to send Denise back to her father's house. The two girls said that they were not worried about Mr. Thompson " 'cause he's cool. He didn't bother us. When he saw us, he just told us to be careful not to be busted by the police." Uncle Charles had told Denise that Mr. Thompson used to smoke marijuana like a chimney and Grandmother Osetta made him stop, but he still drank ganja-rum. According to Denise, after she learned how to smoke marijuana properly, her Uncle Charles was no longer "mad" if she and her womanish girls took some of his herb.

Denise saw her involvement with illicit drugs as a kind of empirical search for the truth. She stated that she wanted to find out the truth about "Nancy Reagan's Just Say No Campaign" (an allusion to the warning about the dangers of marijuana smoking), because the people she knew who smoked marijuana did not say that it was dangerous. Indeed, the overwhelming majority—nearly 90 percent—of respondents in the youth survey confirmed Denise's skepticism about the dangers of smoking marijuana. "It's confusing you know," she said, "when the government says one thing and your people say another." I asked her what she thought the truth was about marijuana, and her response was: "[At that time] me no know. Me can't believe weh me hear or read. Me just waan make sure."

Besides marijuana and crack, Denise had also experimented with mescaline. Because she used to live in Metropolitan Central City, her network of friends extended beyond the geographical boundaries of Fayerville, and she was aware of drugs that were not common in Southland, such as mescaline, which is extracted from the peyote cactus. It is a hallucinogenic drug that was found among Puerto Rican youths in South Fairfield, but not among Blacks in Fayerville. Denise introduced mescaline to her girlfriends in Southland, and she described her experience with this drug to me:

> The first time I popped a mesk [mescaline] tab was a few months after my first smoke of doobie blunt [marijuana rolled up inside a cigar]. Me and my girlfriends—Daphne, Donna, Darlene, Paulette, Paula—and a lot of girls that hang out on the block, we decided to pop a mesk tab so we went to the park farthest away from Wayward Street, where there was not many people, to spend most

of the night outside simply buggin'. Everybody was in a good mood, just happy, talking, laughing.

Once, I couldn't take it outside no more so I walked home. When I got home, I stayed up all night watching TV and buggin' out in my head but at least I felt safe. My grandmother was home already. She opened her door slightly and saw me go into my room. I was like standing in front of the TV and she came in and said "Where you been?" I didn't say nothin', I just stood there staring at her. She makes me nervous looking at me like that, but tonight I didn't flinch. I stood there in front of the TV. After a while she shook her head and left. . . .

Although she was using drugs on a regular basis and drinking alcohol occasionally, Denise rarely sold drugs directly. She had assisted with selling drugs as a steerer (an assistant who solicits potential buyers or brings in new customers) because of her uncanny ability to spot undercover police officers. This is why her nickname on the streets was "Sixth Sense." She used to boast that since she had been hanging out on the streets "not once have me sent 'the man' to any of them [drug] dealers me deal with." The drug dealer (or seller) generally paid her for her services, but occasionally the buyer would give her money or some of the drugs as a gratuity. Denise usually sold any drugs she was given because she felt it was too dangerous to keep drugs on her person. Nonetheless, rumors persisted that she was a drug dealer, to which she responded:

> I do not make me money from [selling] drugs. I'm no drug dealer, I just tell them people where to go to get what them want. Sometimes I'd go get it for them, and them give me money, but I'm not making money selling drugs. The Jamaicans who talk to my father 'n go tell my mother in Kingston that I'm selling drugs, they don't know what they talking about. They so stupid, running their mouth all over the place, frightening my mother.
>
> I don't like Jamaicans 'cause they are nosy people, them always wanna be in yuh business. Me ya tell them off. This is America, man! Central City, not Kingston. It's none of their business. I don't do this [steering] for a living. I don't not even keep them drugs on me body.

Denise was careful not to handle large quantities of illicit drugs because she knew that, if she were caught, she could be charged with intent to distribute narcotics, which was likely to bring a severe sentence. However, if she were caught with small amounts for personal use, she could escape being sent to prison. As Denise became more deeply involved with drug activities, she and her close friend, Daphne, agreed to deliver a large sum of money to a female contact in Fort Lauderdale, Florida. They brought back, to an acquaintance in a borough in Central City, a package thought to contain cocaine. They claimed not to know how much money was in the bag they took to the contact in Florida or what kind of drug that was in the package they brought back to Central City. They said that they did not mind being kept in the dark because that was a precaution to help reduce their sentences should they be arrested, tried, and found guilty. For this task they were each paid $500 and given extra money for the train fare and accommodations. Denise and Daphne insisted that they acted as couriers mainly for the fun of it: to see sunny Florida (and visit Disney World), and to spend some time with relatives and friends who had moved down there. But they also admitted that receiving $500 was an extra incentive.

While preparing for a second trip to Florida, Denise was arrested. She was carrying a bag that contained approximately $10,000, according to the police, but there were no drugs on her. However, it was soon determined that the money was the proceeds from illicit drug sales. Therefore, Denise was charged with belonging to a drug ring and with conspiracy to distribute narcotics. At first she gave the arresting officers false personal information. She told them that she was homeless and inflated her age to 19, although she was not quite 17 years old at the time. As a result, she was kept in the county jail, north of Green Meadows.

JAIL AND PROBATION

Denise recalled an incident in the county jail that she said affected her immensely and perhaps changed her perception of people involved with illegal drugs. According to Denise, as soon as she joined the other female inmates they told her stories about the male correction officers and what to do to curry their favor. For example, she was told not to seal the holes in the bathroom that enabled the male correction officers to peep at the female inmates while they were taking showers. Also, she learned about a "handsome, decent" Jamaican officer called Mr. Reynolds. Denise claimed that all the female prisoners were in love with Mr. Reynolds, not because of his physical appearance but because he treated them as human beings, with respect. According to

Denise, he did not engage in the "Peeping Tom" activities of the younger male correction officers.

The next day, when Denise saw Mr. Reynolds down the hall from her cell, she called to him. She said that she wanted to ask him to inform her Uncle Charles about her arrest because she was afraid to call her father, but felt that someone in the family should know about her situation. However, Mr. Reynolds refused to talk to her; instead he shamed her by saying, "I don't speak to criminals." Denise was shocked by his response because she had heard that he treated the inmates with respect. Denise said she could not easily overcome the hurt of Mr. Reynolds's remark; she cried for the rest of the day. She explained that she was offended by Mr. Reynolds's suggestion that she had become a criminal like the American girls. Apparently, she was baffled that Mr. Reynolds could be on good speaking terms with some of the "most disgusting [American] girls" and yet kept his distance from the West Indian female inmates. Denise maintained that, prior to this incident, she did not consider a person involved with drugs to be a criminal.

Actually, Mr. Reynolds was not from Jamaica, but Barbados. As a member of the Caribbean Islands Association, he knew Denise's father, so when he got home that night, he called Glen to inform him of Denise's arrest. Glen rushed to see his daughter the next morning. He hired an attorney to represent her and thereby released the public defendant who had been assigned to her case. It was Denise's private attorney who worked out a deal with the district attorney; as a result, the more serious charge—conspiracy to distribute narcotics—was dropped. She was sentenced to three to five years in jail on the other charge, but served just five months before being released and placed on probation for six years. A probationary condition for her release from jail was that she return to her parents' home.

Although Rosemary consented to her stepdaughter's return, when Denise got back home from jail, Rosemary did not treat her as a regular member of the household. According to Denise, the only communication between the two of them was when Rosemary would say "hi" to her in the morning and again in the evening, when Rosemary came back from work. Denise expressed an awareness of having brought shame on her family, but added, "She [Rosemary] could have talked to me." Rosemary admitted to not talking to her stepdaughter regularly because, she said, Denise continued to wear "offensive" clothing, such as oversized tee shirts with inscriptions like "I luv my attitude problem," "Central City: Dance or Die," "Give Racism the Boot," and so on. When I asked Denise why she wore these tee shirts, her response was:

"They make me feel good about myself. I like them 'cause I get compli-
ments when I wear them." Another tee shirt she often wore had a portrait of Bob Marley with a marijuana joint in his hand. She explained
that she had been wearing similar types of tee shirts since she was 13.

Her refusal to stop wearing these shirts was another source of tension between her and her stepmother, because Rosemary interpreted
the wearing of a marijuana tee shirt to mean that she was endorsing
the product. Denise disagreed, saying that it was just a tee shirt and
there were no hidden messages involved. Also, whenever Denise quar-
reled with her stepmother she would begin to sing aloud the Bob Marley song, "Get Up Stand Up." If Rosemary were to ask her to tone it
down, Denise would respond angrily, "Me kaan sin' a song in mine father's house? What is this, a concentration camp?" Privately, her father Glen seemed to side with his daughter on this particular issue, but
he refused to be dragged into the quarrel between Denise and Rosemary, insisting that Denise must obey "her mother." Glen's decision
not to become embroiled in the disagreement between his daughter
and wife left the tension between Denise and Rosemary unresolved;
so, about a month after her release from jail, Denise ran away.

While on probation she could not return to her grandmother's
house (her grandmother did not want her to live there), so Denise
temporarily became an "invisible homeless" person (someone who is
not living in a shelter but has no permanent address). After her release from the county jail, she had been "debriefed" by friends and
neighbors who had experienced the criminal justice system. These
people advised her "how to beat the system," that is, how to keep from
getting in trouble for noncompliance with all the terms of her probation. Denise kept a low profile while she reported regularly to her probation officer. If the probation department knew that Denise was
failing to comply with the conditions for her release, not much fuss
was made about it. The probation department was overloaded with
cases, and it was not uncommon for cases to fall through the cracks, so
long as the probationers stayed out of trouble and kept a low profile.

During the month or so that she had lived in her father's house, she
had stayed indoors and watched television most of the time. When she
left to live with her friends and acquaintances in Central City, she still
stayed indoors most of the time but resumed smoking marijuana with increased intensity—four or more times every day. She went on a smoking
binge with Jamaican girlfriends who visited her because, she explained,

> I was depressed and bored . . . I don't like watching soaps or [talk
> shows on TV] that much. Me and Daphne, we just listened to the

> radio playing our [Caribbean] music. I like American music, Rap, R&B, and that kinda music, but after a while it gets kinda boring. I prefer Caribbean and African music 'cause you get variety, lots of variety, man. That's how I dealt with it, listening to music and smoking blunts with my girlfriends.

Denise realized that it was time to find employment to earn regular income as well as to occupy herself. She was bored watching television, so she decided to look for work as a cashier in a supermarket or a fast food restaurant such as McDonald's. However, the process of applying for a job could be intimidating for a high school dropout who had served time in jail and had no marketable skills, and she was turned off. Besides, it was not at all certain that she could fit into a regular work environment because she had scoffed continuously at the idea of working at McDonald's; she derided her schoolmates in work uniforms and sharply criticized their acquiescence to work rules. "Why musta I show respect to customers who do not deserve respect?" she asked rhetorically. Denise was very confrontational and admitted that perhaps she could not function in an establishment with a strict code of conduct such as McDonald's. She gave others the impression that the virtues of the business community were antithetical to her own beliefs and practices.

It was during the time Denise was living with friends that she met the father of her son and soon became pregnant, thus changing her social status and responsibilities. All the members of Denise's inner circle of girlfriends had babies when they were in their teens, except those who went to college, like Michelle. At 18, Denise was actually the last one of the "womanish girls" to become a mother. Not surprisingly, she got pregnant in circumstances related to drug and alcohol use. She said it was an accident, and that there was no real love between her and the baby's father when it happened. She had attended a birthday party at her girlfriend Priscilla's house in South Fairfield. There, they smoked marijuana blunts and drank Cisco, a beer-like alcoholic beverage. Then, according to Denise,

> This Puerto Rican guy, the cousin of Priscilla, my girlfriend, he tried to get busy with me on the sofa in front of everybody. I told him off that he is crazy. He followed me to the bathroom, the kitchen, everywhere I went. When it was time for me to go home, he followed me into the hallway; that's where it happened. I musta been blacked out or something, 'cause I don't remember anythin', nothin', except that I took a gypsy cab back to Fayerville. . . . Yeah, I had seen him before but I didn't know or care for him [her baby's father]. It was just that one time, and I got pregnant.

MOTHERHOOD

Denise gave birth to a baby boy under unusual circumstances. She was visiting friends and shopping in Metropolitan Central City when she first began to have contractions. She said she did not know what was wrong with her but managed to walk to her girlfriend's house nearby, and although Priscilla was not home, her parents let Denise inside. She told them that she was tired and wanted to lie down a little to regain her strength. They allowed her to lie down in Priscilla's room, and according to Denise, "the baby just popped out." She did not know what to do, and as she lay there thinking, the door suddenly opened slightly and she saw Priscilla's grandmother. The elderly woman, thinking that all the crying she heard was from the TV, asked Denise to lower the volume. But the noise was the cry of a real baby, still bloody and screaming, lying on the bed. Priscilla's parents hurriedly called an ambulance, which rushed Denise and her new baby to North General Hospital.

While in the hospital, Denise did not call her relatives. Instead she called her caseworker who directed her to take a cab to a shelter for teenage mothers, located in a neighboring city, once she was discharged from the hospital. Then she called my office and left a message about the birth of Curry and where she would be staying temporarily upon release from the hospital. I immediately visited them at the hospital and suggested that she return to her grandmother's house. Although she said that she was feeling homesick and would like to return to her old neighborhood in Southland, she refused because she feared that her Grandmother Osetta would attempt to have Curry taken away from her.

I got in touch with the chairman of the board of directors of Low-Income Housing and Economic Project, Inc., who knew Denise's father very well. It was decided to get her admitted to the relatively newly constructed homeless shelter near Grandmother Osetta's house. Although this homeless shelter had a long waiting list, a place was secured for Denise, and in two weeks' time Denise and her baby moved to the homeless shelter a few blocks from her grandmother's house. Meanwhile, I contacted Denise's former best girlfriend, Michelle, who returned home immediately from college to give her friend support and to talk to her about returning to her grandmother's house, reassuring Denise that it was okay to return home. However, Grandmother Osetta insisted that Denise sign adoption papers to give

Curry away before she could return home. Denise refused to give up her son for adoption and remained in the homeless shelter, but she visited her grandmother's house regularly.

The birth of Curry had rekindled the fading friendship between Denise and Michelle, whose following remarks accurately sum up Denise's struggle to assume her new role as mother as well as the continuing struggle between her and Grandmother Osetta and Aunt Cherry, the current most significant female relatives in her life.

> I really feel bad to see Denise as a teen mother. All the girls in our group in high school became teenage mothers except Denise and I. But I had not kept in touch with her [Denise] that much 'cause I'm in college and I'm so happy with the new world I'm in. After she gave birth to Curry I saw her trying to be a mother but she was still a young girl and she needed a little help from her aunt [Cherry] and grandmother [Osetta]. But, they [her family] put her down all the time. She would take the baby home [to her grandmother's house] and try to bathe or dress him but they won't let her. I remember when she came to visit me at college in Long Island. She wanted to come with Curry but her aunt wouldn't let her. Anything Denise did, either she was doing it wrong or she just couldn't. Many times I heard her saying "let me do it! I'm his mother! He's my baby." But her aunt would say "that's not how you do it! You don't know what you're doing. No! You can't take him out!" Soon I didn't hear Denise protesting much when they would snatch her son out of her hands. She had no say in anything that had to do with her baby so she resumed hanging out on the streets more often, getting home late and therefore leaving Curry to sleep with Grandmother Osetta, no one said anything because her aunt or grandmother would be taking care of the baby and she was not needed. After a while she wouldn't even go to her grandmother's house, and for a couple of weeks she did not see her son. . . .

CONCLUSION

The case of Denise appears to present a confusing picture: It seems that her peers—the so-called womanish girls—were responsible for her involvement in illegal drug activities. Rosemary was convinced this was the case, and this factor is crucial and played a major role in re-

moving her from her parents' home and relocating her in grandmother's house. Certainly their influence on Denise cannot be denied;
however, peer pressure is not the most important factor in the process
of her becoming involved with drugs. There are more fundamental factors such as family fault lines that preceded her meeting the womanish
girls and her introduction to street life with the Jamaican emphasis.

I argue that the more important factor in Denise becoming a drug
user is her perception of drugs that she developed at home. Her perception was based, to a large extent, on the attitude of her adult relatives toward drugs. Denise's natural mother smoked marijuana
regularly in her native Jamaica before Denise was conceived. In addition, Denise said that before coming to the United States she had observed some of her maternal uncles smoke marijuana, though her
desire to try it began following her observations of her Uncle Charles.

Grandmother Osetta realized that her granddaughter's problems—dropping out of school, illegal drug use, teen pregnancy—went
beyond peer pressure and that solutions to prevent these types of
problems were possible, although not simple. Grandmother Osetta
was of the opinion that these young people are "children at risk,
[therefore] the solution is not in sending them to jail. Rather we going
to have to provide lots of love, jobs, and opportunities [education] for
these children." Grandmother Osetta believed that with the support
of parents, the community, and the government, young women like
Denise could make it in this neighborhood. This 63-year-old grandmother expressed the view that "[drug abuse] is one important ele-
ment of a multitude of problems we have in our community. . . . [they]
include illiteracy, poor health, lack of affordable housing, lack of jobs
that pay well, discrimination, and a host of others." Although Grandmother Osetta did not want drugs to be legalized, she was, at the same
time, reluctant to advocate more stringent drug laws because, as she
put it, "any [policy] is a fiasco if it isn't backed up by honest people."
Like most Southland residents she thought that the police were cor-
rupt; she criticized the criminal justice system for being discriminatory
against Black folks, especially Black youths.

CHAPTER 7

Liz
The Culture Broker

The case of Liz shows a young African-American woman who has chosen not to use or sell illegal drugs; get pregnant during her teenage years, as most of her friends did; or drop out of school. I present her case not simply as a counterexample to the others, but more important, to search for answers to questions such as: Why is she so resilient? What makes certain individuals not succumb to the pressures that destroy those around them? Is Liz's success influenced by her parents' strong marriage, by not being an out-of-wedlock baby herself, by having a father in the home, by not being as lackadaisically supervised as my other informants? Her portrait suggests several factors, but before discussing them, let me first recount how I met her.

I met 19-year-old Liz Payne while doing my dissertation research in 1990. I had gone to her mother's secondhand clothing and furniture store to look for space to rent as an office for my field operations. Liz was a freshman at a community college in a neighboring county, but had come home for spring break. When she heard me talk to her mother about my research, she became interested and volunteered to

135

participate in it because "It sounds so interesting. . . . I've never done drugs but I can tell you a lot about it [drug use and dealing] here in Fayerville. I know a lot of kids that do drugs; they are my friends."

I welcomed her willingness to introduce me to her friends, but was reluctant to include her as a subject in the study because my plan was to focus on young people who were involved with drugs—users and dealers. She made a compelling argument, but what really changed my mind were the comments made by her mother, Mrs. Sylvia Payne, a well-respected religious leader and local businesswoman who had managed to see her only child graduate from Fayerville High School and now attend college. Sister Payne, as she is affectionately called, expressed concerns about my study that other local residents also expressed. She questioned my decision to focus only on young men and women who use or sell illegal drugs and pleaded that her daughter be included in my study:

> Why do you have to concentrate on only the few bad apples? Why do you want to focus only on the negatives? Why aren't you interested in positive things in our [Black] community? [My daughter] knows the kids you are looking for, the kids who use and sell drugs. She grew up with them; they went to school together; they come to the store all the time. . . . She will introduce them to you, but why only them? Not all kids in our community use drugs. Not all kids in our community are drug dealers or crackheads. When are you going to study the good kids, the ones who do not use or sell drugs? The ones who do not prostitute themselves, but go to church every Sunday? We have beautiful [good] young men and women, too, in our community. You should include them in your study.

I decided then and there to include her 19-year-old daughter as a subject in my study. At the time, I was not fully aware of the import of my decision. It was obvious from the start that Liz could provide an interesting contrast to those who were engaged in illegal drug activities, but I had not given much thought beyond that. In retrospect, however, I realize that Liz's inclusion offered more than a contrast between Black youths involved with illegal drugs (users and dealers) and those who were not involved.

After I had interviewed and observed Liz several times, I discovered that she possessed a keen sense of what was happening in her neighborhood; she was truly a perceptive observer of the social scene in Fayerville. She espoused a remarkably balanced view of the generational "tug-of-war" between her own generation and that of her parents.[1] Even though Liz abstained from illegal drug use, her peers involved with drugs trusted her, and very few of them expressed resentment toward her conventional ways. Also, her participation in this study helped me bring into focus the significant role persons of mixed ethnic backgrounds play within the Black community.

SOCIAL RELATIONSHIPS

Liz is from an ethnically mixed parentage. Her mother came from St. Croix, part of the Virgin Islands in the Caribbean, and her father, Mr. Fred Payne, was from the state of Alabama. So she grew up in a household of African-American and West Indian influences. Even though she told me that she felt closer to her maternal relatives (West Indians) than to her paternal relatives (African Americans), when asked, she nevertheless identified herself as an American, not as a West Indian. She was, however, quick to add: "It's not because I dis[respect] them. No! I'm proud of my West Indian heritage and I love to go to St. Croix for vacation, but the fact of the matter is I was born right here in the United States." Interestingly, Liz's father downplayed his identity as an American and emphasized his affinal relationship to West Indians. When I first met Mr. Payne, he stressed the fact that both his wife and daughter were from the West Indies, which momentarily made me think that Liz might be either his stepdaughter or an adopted child.

Liz's decision to present herself as an American, instead of a West Indian, reflects her deep emotional attachment as well as strong practical ties to the United States. She was born and raised in the Southland neighborhood, where she attended public schools (except for one academic year that she spent with her maternal grandparents in St. Croix while her mother was gravely ill and could not care for her), and most of Liz's girlfriends lived in Fayerville.

Soon after completing my dissertation research, the Payne family relocated to St. Croix[2] and Liz transferred to the College of U.S. Virgin Islands, where she obtained an associate's degree that enabled her to work as a dental technician. I thought she might have difficulty deciding where to settle after receiving her degree, but that was not the case. She realized that the United States offered better employment opportunities than the island of St. Croix, and she returned to Fayerville. Liz plans to go back to school to get a bachelor's degree, but in the meantime she works as a dental assistant in the Northside of town. Liz is very close to her parents (closer than many of her girlfriends are to their own parents), so it was a surprise that she left them in St. Croix and returned to Fayerville.

Liz was a little girl when her father managed a local strip-joint called "Zululand." Her parents told me that, at that time, they both smoked marijuana daily. However, Liz does not recall seeing her parents smoke marijuana, but she remembers a few occasions when they were intoxicated. Upon becoming born-again Christians, Mr. and Mrs. Payne had given up drinking and drug use. They even objected to tenants smoking in their house. According to Mrs. Payne, this prohibition is more a health and safety precaution than a moral imposition. (In the mid-1980s, when crack came on the drug scene, the Southland community experienced a rash of fires that the fire department attributed to careless smoking by persons under the influence of crack.)

The Payne family lived in a big house in the notorious drug-infested area dubbed the Jamaican Alley by African-American neighbors.[3] At one time they rented rooms to boarders who mostly were single men. According to Mrs. Payne, these men would hold parties on weekends that lasted until the wee hours of Sunday morning. She also accused them of excessive drinking and drug use, as well as bringing into the building unsavory characters (prostitutes). Sometimes the partying degenerated into fistfights and the police were called to the Paynes' house many times. Yet Mrs. Payne insisted it was her family's newfound religion that influenced them to stop renting rooms to boarders. Instead she converted the rooms into apartments for families (women) with children. At the time I first visited them, there were four families, including the Payne family, occupying the house, which was originally built for just two families. Rumor had it that the conversion was illegal, but the authorities had not taken action against the Paynes because of an acute shortage of housing in Fayerville.

Liz and her parents occupied the first-floor apartment; the second- and third-floor apartments, as well as the basement apartment, were rented to tenants with large families. The Payne family and their tenants did not constitute a single household unit because they did not interact on a regular basis; the tenants used a separate (back-door) entrance to their apartments. I did not observe any sustained social interaction between Liz and the tenants and therefore concluded that the tenants had no appreciable influence on Liz's life, and vice versa.

The Payne family, unlike other families in the neighborhood, was small, consisting of only Liz and her parents. It was a nuclear family in the classic sense of the term. However, during the summer months this nuclear family expanded into an extended family when Mrs. Payne's relatives came from St. Croix for vacation. Occasionally, the Payne family would host a church member in need of temporary housing or shelter, because their apartment was relatively large. It had three bedrooms, a living room, a kitchen, a dining room, a bathroom, and a small utility room. There was also a foyer that was converted into a sleeping area during the hot summer months. The Paynes' apartment was furnished with expensive carpeting and furniture. A visitor could not miss noticing the religious symbols and artifacts that decorated the rooms. Also, the Paynes' home was equipped with modern household appliances such as a large refrigerator, a microwave oven, a washing machine and dryer, a stereo system, and two color televisions, as well as wall-to-wall carpeting and an old piano that was rarely used. There was always food cooking on the stove, as Mr. and Mrs. Payne liked to entertain visitors with food and nonalcoholic beverages.

When she talked about the seemingly intractable socioeconomic problems facing the Southland community, Mrs. Payne was philosophical in casting blame. She said, "It's not the community but the people [residents] in this neighborhood . . . just like this building [she pointed to a dilapidated apartment building across the street] it's the tenants living in it and not the building itself that's the problem." She complained that many Southland residents no longer showed interest in rebuilding their once vibrant, thriving, model-city community. She regretted the loss of a sense of community that was palpable when she first arrived in this neighborhood from her native St. Croix in the 1970s. To improve living conditions in Southland, Mrs. Payne advocated finding a way to promote better communication among residents and encourage them to take pride in this community once again. Both she and Liz regretted the political schism that had developed between West Indians and African Americans and talked about how the lack of cooperation could weaken the Black vote in municipal elections. The Paynes wanted to build a bridge between African Americans and West Indians and felt that many storefront churches in this community should be promoted by this goal.

Liz maintained good relations with a number of significant adults, mostly members of her church—the Church of Holy Communion. However, her social life was by no means circumscribed by her in-

volvement with her church. She interacted regularly with other significant adults, such as her Aunt Felicia, the half-sister of her mother.
Aunt Felicia was not particularly religious; she attended church services only on such special occasions as Easter and Christmas or for
marriages, christenings, and funerals. Aunt Felicia's home, which was
located on the Northside of town, could be described as a secular
household. It consisted of Aunt Felicia; Philippe, her Haitian husband; and their 10-month-old son, Pierre. Liz adored her little cousin,
Pierre, whom she often babysat. When asked whether she intended to
have children, Liz's immediate response was, "Yes, of course! I want
to have kids 'cause I love children. They are adorable." Then she
quickly added, "Not any time soon, [however], 'cause first I have to
[be certain of] what I'm going to do after I finish college. I would like
to get married so that my children will have a father at home." Although Liz got along well with her Aunt Felicia (whom she described
as her favorite aunt), she maintained that Aunt Felicia was "a little
too materialistic" for her. Liz admired Aunt Felicia for her good taste,
charm, and effervescence, but also the fortitude and industriousness
of her mother (Mrs. Payne) impressed her greatly. In addition, she
found the "street smarts" of her father to be very appealing because,
as she put it, "In America you can't get ahead if you ain't tough and
street smart [clever]." Aunt Felicia complained that Liz's parents
were concerned about her niece's frequent visits to her (Aunt Felicia's) home because her husband occasionally smoked marijuana with
his friends. However, Liz's parents denied this, saying that they
trusted their daughter. Liz said that her mother expressed the concern
just once.

Liz associated with many people who were not religiously inclined; these people were mainly African American and West Indian.
Some of them used and/or sold illegal drugs regularly. Liz's parents
encouraged her to associate with a cross-section of the community because, according to Mrs. Payne, they wanted her to be "comfortable
with people different from her." However, another reason is that her
parents thought it would prepare her for a future as a missionary in
the Third World. I asked Mrs. Payne about allowing her daughter to
associate with young women and men with questionable reputations,
and her response was that she and her husband trusted their daughter
to "take care of herself . . . she will not do what she is not supposed to
do." Liz knows that her parents put confidence and trust in her and is
determined not to let them down. Many neighbors say that her parents' trust and confidence are key ingredients in the good relationship

that exists between Liz and her parents. I would like to add that trust and confidence were key in keeping Liz from becoming a drug user or dealer. Her parents had given her a challenge and she was determined not to fail.

Even though Liz associated with many people, she was close to only a few of them, whom she described as "friends" or "close associates." According to Liz, a friend or a close associate is someone in whose home she would voluntarily stay overnight or whose clothes she would borrow for an outing. I used these criteria to determine that Liz had just four girlfriends or close associates. They included a 30-year-old mother of three young children, named Jackie, who used and sold drugs before she met the Payne family; 18-year-old Samantha, who admitted to experimenting with marijuana while in high school; Cynthia, who, like Liz, was a 19-year-old college student who claimed never to have used or sold drugs; and 15-year-old Valerie, who did not want to become involved with drugs because of her "big sister's" (Liz's) positive influence. Liz did not have a boyfriend after her breakup with Dread because, as she put it, "as far as I'm concerned, if you are a Christian and you have a boyfriend, husband, lover, or whatever, who doesn't want to be saved, turn him loose. You don't need a man who doesn't want to go to church." Despite these strong sentiments, Liz maintained contact with her ex-boyfriend, Dread, and she recruited him for this study.

LIZ'S CAREER CHOICES

Liz would like to get ahead in America but is uncertain about her career path. At the time I met Liz, Mr. Payne worked as a dental technician in a laboratory located on Wayward Street, across the street from his wife's secondhand furniture and clothing store. Besides being a dental technician, Mr. Payne spent a lot of time, as an elder, attending to the affairs of the Church of Holy Communion. On the second Sunday of every month he visited the county jail as a missionary. Both Liz and Mrs. Payne accompanied him on the trip.

Like her father, she now works as a dental technician but says, "I do not want to be a dental technician all my life." She wants a career that is spiritually rewarding but one that would also provide her with material comfort and security. She thought about majoring in business

to enhance her chances of working for a major corporation and earning a handsome salary. However, she is concerned that her friends in
her church would put her down. In the past, when she talked to them
about pursuing a professional career to make a lot of money, they criticized her harshly, accusing her of selfishness and putting personal de-
sires above serving God. Liz denies that her intention is to abandon
serving God. She insists that she wants to serve God but would like to
do so without sacrificing the comforts of earthly life; she is determined
to improve her family's standard of living. Her other friends who are
not religiously inclined think "it's cool, making all that crazy money."

During a trip to an amusement park in another city, Liz talked to
me candidly about her anxieties regarding the high expectations her
parents had of her. She was the first member of her extended family
to attend college, an accomplishment that had already given her and
her parents prestige and recognition among relatives and neighbors in
St. Croix. She volunteered as a youth leader in her church, and the
congregation considered her a "rising star." The church's elderly
women spoke in laudatory terms about her maturity, generosity, and
good deeds, such as teaching Sunday school and accompanying her
parents to minister to inmates in the county jail. A middle-aged
church member, who sacrificed a college education to raise a family,
said about Liz, "She hasn't let college get into her head as some of you
[college-educated] do, you know?" After graduating from high school
Liz considered becoming a missionary in Africa or India, so she attended a religious academy for a year and earned a diploma. However, she changed her mind because she was concerned that
missionary work would not earn her enough money to live comfortably. Therefore, she enrolled at a community college with the intention of majoring in business. After she took a course in government,
however, Liz changed her mind again and decided to major in political science. She asked me about career opportunities for political science majors and thought of going to law school or to graduate school
for a master's in public administration, in order to pursue a public service career. However, all of that changed when her family moved to
the U.S. Virgin Islands.

Mr. and Mrs. Payne had other ideas for their only daughter. They
wanted her to pursue a career in the ministry, "to spread the word of
Our Lord Jesus Christ," as Mrs. Payne put it. Mrs. Payne, in particular, dismissed her daughter's concern about the inadequate salary for
working in the ministry. In order to explain, Liz mentioned an incident
involving her father, an ordained minister. Mr. Fred Payne often as-

sumed speaking engagements in the neighboring Central City. He had recently spoken to a Pentecostal congregation and was given an honorarium of about $200. He turned over the entire sum to his church, saying that "as a church elder it's the proper thing to do." His church did not demand that he donate this money to its coffers, he did it voluntarily because he wanted to set a good example. Liz rejected her father's magnanimity, explaining that she did not object to the idea of contributing a tenth of her income to the church, as all members were required to do, but then she spoke out against turning over one's entire secondary earnings to the church, as her father did. Furthermore, she did not think it was fair. Mrs. Payne rejected their daughter's criticism and supported her husband's actions, believing that if one gave generously to the Church of Holy Communion, God would find a way to reward one with more money.

LIZ AND HER PARENTS

Mrs. Payne's faith and enthusiasm in the church bordered on fanaticism. She was always proselytizing, trying to recruit new members from the ranks of the downtrodden, the most vulnerable in this community, such as drug addicts, alcoholics, ex-convicts, and homeless mothers. That was how she recruited 30-year-old Jackie, a former addict who sold drugs to supplement her family's income. When Jackie's boyfriend was killed in a shootout a few years back, Mrs. Payne gave her and her children shelter for about two months. It was during that time that Jackie and Liz became close friends. Much of Liz's street smarts and insight about the world of drug users and dealers was gained from Jackie.

Liz opposed her mother's efforts to pressure Jackie to give a tenth of her welfare monetary assistance to the Church of Holy Communion. Liz encouraged Jackie not to acquiesce because "the $600 a month stipend [public assistance] Jackie receives is barely sufficient to take care of her and her three kids." Therefore, argued Liz, Jackie should be exempted from the obligatory donation to the church. Sister Payne disagreed, saying:

> Oh no! Jackie can give a tenth of her [welfare] check to the church because she pays no rent. She gets chapter eight [implying that her rent is paid for her]. A lot of people on welfare waste

their money buying "junk," [an allusion to a stereotype of welfare
mothers]. Jackie wastes lots of money on junk . . . she knows that
I know this because she is like [part of our] family. . . . God will
give [to] her, will reward her many times over if she donates to
the church.

Even though Liz and her mother disagreed on some issues, they
were careful not to let the disagreements disrupt their friendship.
Both mother and daughter describe their relationship as "the best of
friends." Mr. Payne agreed, saying that his wife was a good role model
for their daughter but added that it was the openness in the relationship between Mrs. Payne and Liz that made it work. Thus, openness,
which he defined as straight-talk, must be part of the formula for raising children properly in the "ghetto." Mrs. Payne told me that Liz is
her "best friend 'cause she is the only child God gave me." Liz recipro-
cated with kind words confirming what her mother said that, indeed,
Mrs. Payne was her confidant. She described their relationship as
"open," meaning she could discuss any subject with her mother without fear of rebuke or retribution.

During the entire period of fieldwork I seldom witnessed heated
discussions or angry exchanges between Liz and her mother. Occasionally, there was tension between mother and daughter. For example,
one afternoon Liz wanted to go shopping with Jackie, but her mother
refused to give her permission because there was much work to complete in the store. After a brief exchange of words, Liz stayed behind
and assisted her mother in completing the tasks. Liz describes her
mother as "authoritarian" (actually she is a disciplinarian), but Liz has
enormous affection and respect for her so that when disagreements
between mother and daughter occurred, they were handled in a nona-
crimonious manner and rarely required the intervention of Mr. Payne.

Neighbors and Liz's friends praise Mr. and Mrs. Payne for doing a
good job in steering Liz away from the many problems teenage girls
faced in this neighborhood. They say that both Mr. and Mrs. Payne
are equally responsible for their daughter's "success" (achievement).
However, Mr. Payne gives all the credit to his wife because, as he put,
"she did all the work [training]." Mr. Payne's reluctance to accept the
credit for keeping his daughter out of trouble is due to the fact that,
although he was always around, it was Mrs. Payne who was most involved in Liz's upbringing. She trained and disciplined their daughter
to "do the right thing," to be socially as well as morally responsible in
her behavior. According to Mr. Payne, he assisted only when called
upon to do so. He described himself as an "old-fashioned kinda guy"

when it came to family or domestic matters. He believed that what occurred at home was the "natural" domain of responsibility of his wife and thus she must assume the task of raising their daughter. However, he maintained that had they had a boy he would have taken a more active role in his training or upbringing.

Mr. Payne generally gave his wife high marks in raising Liz, but felt that sometimes she was not as firm as she should be when disciplining Liz. He talked about an incident involving his wife and their daughter to illustrate his point. He said that sometimes when Liz did something wrong, Mrs. Payne would order her to stop watching TV and go to bed, even if it was not yet time to go to sleep. Liz would disregard this order and continue to watch television. Her mother would not insist on her going to bed until she did something else that irritated Mrs. Payne; then she would shout at her: "Didn't I ask you to go to bed?" and again Liz would disregard the order. At this point Mrs. Payne would call Mr. Payne to come and discipline Liz, but often her husband's response was very brief: "Say what you mean and mean what you say." Mr. Payne explained that Mrs. Payne's half-hearted measures suggested that she did not want Liz to go to bed; rather, the punishment was "telling" her to go to bed. Then he added: "If you mean to tell her to go to bed you must insist and stop her from watching the television and see to it that she goes to her bedroom. If you want to punish her for something she did, don't confuse her by [merely] saying she must go to bed."

Liz and her mother criticized young people who did not graduate from high school. Liz agreed with her mother that young people needed help to cultivate the appropriate behavior adults expected of them. Adults should therefore be on constant vigil to prevent them from slipping: "We must help them along as they try to develop habits of appropriate behavior and avoid those behaviors that are socially reprehensible." According to Mrs. Payne, the secret for raising good kids in a tough neighborhood like Southland is that parents (or guardians) should make it their first priority and they must be firm but at the same time fair in their relationship with their children.

"Without the love and support of my parents," she said, "I would have been out there on the streets just like the other girls you've been talking to." While Liz maintained that talking things over with her mother was the single most significant factor in preventing her from becoming a "statistic" (dead) like some girls who were murdered or who overdosed on drugs, she credited her father for making her aware of and therefore less vulnerable to the "sweet nothing talk" of men,

which helped her to avoid "sexual exploitation" by men in this community. She said that she had learned a great deal about men from listening to stories told by her father, whose former reputation as a
womanizer was not unknown to his daughter.

ATTITUDE TOWARD DRUGS

Southland, with its abandoned buildings, overcrowded homes, and
drug-selling activities, was the neighborhood in which Liz grew up—
an environment that was no different for her than for many of the
young women who became involved with drugs. Thus, what accounts
for Liz's abstinence from drugs? Certainly, the fact that she was the
only child and was the center of attention of *both* her parents played a
significant role. Also, both of her parents *formerly* had been active on
the drug scene and they constantly spoke out about using drugs to
their daughter from that experience. As well, her family's involvement
with the Church of Holy Communion served as a disincentive for Liz
to become involved with drugs. Mrs. Payne believed that Liz's active
participation in the church's activities left her no time to "fool
around" with drugs or boys and it helped to keep her off the streets.
Liz truly enjoyed her active involvement with the Church of Holy
Communion. She explained her attraction to this church this way: "I
like the music, the singing . . . in the church we make lots of noise."
Mrs. Payne strongly believed that it was the Lord Jesus Christ who
saved their daughter from the destructive behaviors of the streets. Liz
did not disagree.

While Liz's church forbade its members from using either drugs
or alcohol, she insisted that her abstinence from drugs or alcohol use
was not a "religious thing." Liz's attitude toward illegal drug use and
alcohol was highly complex; she did not condemn those involved with
drugs or alcohol, yet she was not neutral on the subject. She believed
that teenagers who used and/or sold drugs were primarily looking for
an opportunity to earn money and status in the community and that
was why she did not condemn them. "It's the American way!" she
once told me. She told associates not to become involved with drugs;
however, if they did become involved, she did not break ties with
them. To understand her attitude, one has to realize that Liz did not
consider drug use alone a sufficient reason to break off a relationship.

Although Liz maintained that she did not use alcohol, she was not quite a teetotaler because, occasionally, she would accept a glass of wine; rather, she found alcoholics (and there are many in this neighborhood) to be "disgusting." In addition, Liz was very health conscious and believed that excessive drinking contributed to poor health. Liz explained that although those who abused drugs or alcohol were sometimes ridiculed and called disparaging names, such as crackhead, junkie, pothead, bum, and so forth, the few drug dealers who made a lot of money often gained a higher social status because of their generosity. For example, Jerome Frazier, a local prizefighter in the 1970s who was known to have become a drug dealer after his fighting days were over, donated large sums of money to the Jerusalem Baptist Church, a small storefront church that was founded and led by his girlfriend's mother. Occasionally, he also gave free frozen turkeys to a few families in Southland who couldn't afford Thanksgiving or Christmas dinner. However, Jerome wasn't the only drug dealer locally known for his generosity. The notorious Nicky Barnes has a reputation in this community for paying for some local young men and women to attend traditionally Black colleges in the South. Jerome and Nicky belong to the old (30 years and over) generation of Black men who sold drugs in this community but also have reputations for their generosity. Among the younger generation Gerald and Dread are quite well known for their generous tips in local restaurants and businesses.

Liz agrees with me that shaming could prevent some of her friends from becoming regularly involved with illegal drugs. She argues that if doing or selling drugs were seen by her peers as not cool, but instead as something that brings shame, then some kids would give up. She maintains that especially the boys in her junior high school used to smoke marijuana to impress the girls. They had reputations as guys you can't mess with and who had money. But if a girl they liked didn't want to be associated with their drug use, they were prepared to give it up. Mrs. Payne said that some of what Liz and I were saying could be true but she did not believe that shaming could be an effective deterrent. "Some of the kids you can shame, but the majority you can't because it [drug use or selling] begins at home." She asked rhetorically, "How are you going to shame me when you [parents] are taking drugs yourself? It's not a single generation, it is all [multiple] generations." She challenged me to investigate the generational use of drugs. "You will find that someone, an adult in the kid's family, used drugs before." She argued that an outsider could not shame children because they would tell her: "You are not my mother, if my mother allows me to do it, who are you to tell me it's bad or wrong?" Jackie, like Mrs. Payne, blamed parents for drug use by their children because they did not set a good example. Jackie was emphatic:

> I feel it's the fault of mothers who are on drugs . . . the kids rule over them. . . . It's a psychological thin', when children see their mothers [or fathers] on crack they lose respect for them. . . . Crack is popular because they [crackheads] think it's gonna take away their problems but the problem gets bigger . . . I know many women like that. I don't get involved with them any more.

As far as Mrs. Payne was concerned, the problem of drug abuse is a moral issue. To her, those who argued that the drug problem was simply a criminal or an economic issue were reluctant to face the real issue. She believed that was why it had not been stamped out of this society. She thought that if drug use were to be recognized fundamentally as a moral issue there would be nowhere else for it "to hide its evil head." According to Mrs. Payne, the most effective way out of the "drug mess" is to be saved by the Lord Jesus Christ.

To discuss this proposition, I asked Jackie (the ex-drug addict and a member of the Church of Holy Communion) about the lack of church-sponsored treatment programs for the many young men and women involved with drugs in this neighborhood. Her response was, "We [churchgoers] don't believe in programs. Jesus Christ is our detox," whereupon both Liz and Mrs. Payne shouted "Amen!" Jackie dismissed drug treatment programs as a waste of time because when a person "graduated" from a therapeutic community he or she went back to drugs within a three-week period. This is how she expressed it:

> A person gets away from rehab and looks clean and fat for eating well during the period he was receiving the so-called treatment. Friends see him on the streets again and tell him you looking fine man; why don't you share a joint with me, here is some crack, it's free, it's on me. The first one, the sample is always free. . . . It's difficult for an ex-addict to turn down something like that, the temptation is too strong, so he takes it, and within three weeks he is back to where he was before rehab.

Jackie sharply criticized group therapy sessions in rehabs as "glorifying the devil in the name of talking about their problem."

Liz believed that most young women in Southland first became involved with drugs primarily through their association with the men they dated. She also pointed out that boyfriends of the young women who became involved with drugs often beat them, but the women seldom called the police. According to Liz, "calling the police will get you into a lot more trouble; they [young women] don't have anybody or anywhere to turn." She considered herself fortunate for having parents who trusted her and on whom she could rely.

I asked her why she did not become involved with drugs, and Liz mentioned certain incidents involving drug use that had great impact on her. For instance, her father was attacked by a sanitation worker that was later found to be under the influence of crack. It happened on a Monday morning when the sanitation truck was on the street in front of the Paynes' house picking up discarded household appliances and furniture. Mr. Payne shouted at a young sanitation worker not to pick up a sofa alone because he could hurt his back. Then he left the porch of his house to give this young man a hand. However, the young man punched Mr. Payne, breaking his jaw. Later the perpetrator said that he thought Mr. Payne had "dis[respected]" him. The violent behavior of that young man who was later labeled a crackhead scared Liz and caused her to believe that crack could turn a smoker instantly into a violent person. Obviously, this is a stereotypical image of a crack smoker, but nevertheless, Liz said it had an impact on her and therefore cannot be ignored. Clearly, the issue of violence associated with drugs is important and must be considered, as Liz seems to imply with the mention of this particular incident.

ATTITUDE TOWARD TEENAGE PREGNANCY

Another problem that concerned Liz as much as drug abuse was teenage pregnancy. She often talked about it because she knew many teenage mothers and the problems they faced raising their children. Asked how she managed to escape pregnancy when many of the girls with whom she grew up have had children, she said:

> Some teenagers think they are ready to be parents; what they don't [realize] is that once you become a parent it's for life, you don't try it out for a while to see if you like it and if you don't you can get your old life back guaranteed [i.e., your youth back].

The following remarks by Liz on the subject demonstrate that she had thought seriously about it and decided that premature pregnancy was not for her:

> It's funny how all the girls I went to school with decided they were
> going to have children and after a year or two they lost interest in
> the babies they brought into this world . . . . They realized they
> had made a mistake by becoming mothers so young, because they
> have so much more to experience before they could give a child
> all he [or she] needed. No, I don't think they were thinking about
> what they could give to their kids. The conclusion I've reached
> about the girls is that they hold their kids responsible for them
> not being able to go out doing everything the rest of the girls their
> age are doing, so once the kids learned to walk and talk and no
> longer depended on them like they did when they were infants,
> out the door they go! Most of the girls I grew up with have kids,
> but it's funny how they're all living the same kind of lives we lived
> when we were 15 or 16.

The relationship between her girlfriends who had turned to drugs
and/or had given birth and their mothers was not close; it was not one
in which the young women sought the advice of their mothers. Liz explained that "mothers could try to understand their daughters a little
more but they won't allow their girls to get too close to them for fear
that the girls may drop the babies in their home and never come
back. . . . You see they [parents] have to know what to do."

Liz made the point over and over again that too many youths in
this city have too much idle time and idleness breeds "trouble." She
was lucky to escape this problem because she worked in her mother's
store and sometimes helped out in her father's laboratory, across the
street from her mother's store. Liz thought that when young girls were
not engaged in work, they welcomed advances from men that almost
always led to intercourse and premature pregnancy.

Another factor contributing to teenage pregnancy, according to
Liz, is that the girls have problems at home and do not know where to
turn for help. Consequently, when young men cross their paths with
"sweet-nothing talk," the girls succumb and eventually the lovemak-
ing results in unplanned pregnancies. As she put it, "girls look for
love, when they [are] catching hell at home; they [are] desperate for
attention, someone to show them love, affection, some understanding,
you know. That's how it happens with most of the girls [teenage moth-
ers] I know."

On the trip to the amusement park, Liz had on a tee shirt with the
inscription "I'm a special person." Her mother had given her the tee
shirt as a birthday present. When asked about the significance of the
inscription, Mrs. Payne said, among other things that, "life is difficult
and you can't accomplish much until you feel good about yourself;

that's what I always tell my daughter that self-esteem comes from within. I want her to feel and believe that she is special."

Conclusion

The success of Liz in not getting involved with illegal drugs or early pregnancy is due to several factors, including the philosophy of "clean living" espoused by her church, her close relationship with her parents, and keeping busy.

While the church taught "clean living" and provided opportunities for Liz to volunteer her time, the most important influence on Liz and the decisions she made was her parents' love and trust. She credits her avoidance of drug use and drug peddling as well as being alive beyond the age of 21 to the confidence and trust that her parents invested in her. In retrospect, Liz said that parental trust guaranteed her the freedom that all human beings, especially kids, sought. She said that her parents constantly warned her that if she did what she was not supposed to do, such as smoke, drink, and have sex, and they found out about it, they would curtail her freedom of movement and association. She avoided doing those things because she did not want to lose her "rights."

She agreed with both her mother and Jackie that Black youths in this neighborhood became involved with drugs primarily because there was nothing for them to do. In other words, they were bored most of the time. Liz did not feel that her life was empty nor was she searching for something to do. In fact, it had become increasingly difficult to "hang out" with friends or date young men because she was busy with studies, she was actively involved with her church, and she helped her mother in the store. She said that she was rarely bored.

Notes

[1] For a fine disquisition on this subject, see Margaret Mead's (1970) *Culture and Commitment: A Study of the Generation Gap*.

[2] Even though Mrs. Payne initiated the decision to return to St. Croix, Mr. Payne wholeheartedly supported it. It's been over a decade since the Paynes relocated to St. Croix, and Mrs. Payne has visited Fayerville several times. However, Mr. Payne has not been back. His friends doubt he will ever return to the United States.

[3] The Paynes' house was located directly across the street from the apartment building in which Dread and his mother, Colleen, lived. The close proximity of their living quarters brought Mrs. Payne and Colleen together and subsequently led to a brief friendship (others say a love affair) between their children, Liz and Dread.

CHAPTER 8

Where Do We Go from Here?

Drug use and sales commonly occur in low-income Black neighborhoods such as Southland. These neighborhoods, popularly known as "inner cities," are also the locus of much of Black people's struggle for political rights, economic opportunity, and social justice in the United States. Members of these communities gradually have been overcome by a profound sense of psychological depression, personal worthlessness, and social despair; they perceive themselves as alienated from mainstream society. A liberal commentator suggests that widespread drug activities in these areas are responsible for the social malaise that threatens the very existence of Black American communities (West 1993).

However, in Southland, the sale or use of illegal drugs is not considered the enemy. This community is more concerned about police brutality (for example, the shooting of the unarmed immigrant from Guinea, Amadou Diallo, who was shot 41 times by police) as well as the police's apparent lack of respect for Black people or peoples of African descent. This is often colloquially expressed as racism or

White supremacy, which Blacks believe is generally responsible for their continued sociopolitical and economic "oppression" in this country. Because Black youths' involvement with drugs may reflect the perceptions of the larger community in which they live, it makes perfect sense to explore the sociocultural context of their drug use.

To understand the full range of issues surrounding Black youths' involvement with illegal drugs, we must move away from models that describe a split society of drug users and non-drug users, thereby disregarding the cultural context of drug use, and shun approaches that narrowly focus on only the users and sellers, thereby ignoring the drug phenomenon as an interactive process. Even the deviant-behavior paradigm, which has dominated drug research for more than four decades, conceptualizes drug use behavior in static, unidimensional terms and leaves little or no room for consideration of the dynamic relationship that exists between drugs, society, and culture. The knowledge and understanding acquired from my decade-long ethnographic investigations in Southland indicate that adopting these approaches is tantamount to scapegoating individual members of the inner-city Black communities.

The alternative cultural-normalization model better serves the purpose of comprehending Black youths' involvement with drugs because it truly reflects social or cultural realities on the ground. Ethnographic research in Southland made evident to me that there are multiple patterns of involvement with illegal drugs in this community, revealed by the five portraits presented here. For example, 19-year-old Liz, with the support of her family and the protection of her religious practice, stubbornly resisted participation in illegal drug activities, yet did not refrain from regular contact or sever social interaction with other youths who used and/or sold illicit drugs. Then there were those, like 20-year-old Akosua, who were involved with drugs but showed no visible signs of severe suffering from social problems generally associated with drug addiction. Sixteen-year-old Gerald and 19-year-old Dread, who were involved with drugs as a means of raising capital in order to start legitimate businesses, also showed minimal social disruption in their daily lives. The stereotypical image of the Black youths involved with drugs most approximated that of 18-year-old Denise whose involvement with illegal drugs was marked by serious social disruptions. But even Denise was not ostracized from the community because of her involvement with drugs per se.

This study has sought to understand the role of culture in attracting inner-city Black youths to illegal drugs when so many of them are already languishing in jails and prisons across the nation as a result of their involvement with drugs. The situation makes you wonder if the young men and women are aware of the consequences of incarceration: Are they not aware of the ramifications of incarceration on a Black person's opportunities in life? Or do they simply not care? Most young people I came across when working in this community tell me of an older relative—a parent, an aunt, an uncle, or an older sibling—doing time in jail for drug-related offences. They see the arrests and incarceration for selling drugs as part of the "deal" for being born Black in White America, to paraphrase Gerald.

There is also a need to focus attention on middle-level institutions, such as the family, ethnic group, community, or social class, which mediate between the individual and the larger society as well as between ethnic minorities and the state (for further discussions see Schensul 1997). What is the role of such institutions in the process of young people becoming involved with illegal drugs? Again, as my findings indicate, the process begins with relatives at home, not with peers on the streets, as conventional wisdom would have it. Blaming youths' involvement with illegal drugs on peer pressure is blaming the victim because it seems to absolve adults from the responsibility of the enforcement of social control. As one of my key informants, Denise, bluntly put it: "Kids and adults all want the same thing, except we [teens] get in trouble for it."

The cultural-normalization model ensures that the emic viewpoints of the locals themselves are obtained. This model offers policymakers the opportunity to realize two elements that seem to be lacking in contemporary democracies: (1) to know what the silent majority in their constituencies is thinking, and (2) to provide insights into the cultural meaning (i.e., the basis) for their thoughts and actions. In this regard, I suggest some relationships between the local community and other social phenomena that illuminate the hidden process of the social construction of meanings—perceptions and understandings of social realities—that are both articulated through individuals' involvement with drugs and projected by social attitudes toward drug use and sale. This kind of understanding will help avoid disastrous policies such as the Rockefeller Laws in New York. These laws failed to serve as a deterrent to the use and sale of drugs because they were formulated by lawmakers who assumed, incorrectly, that jail time means the same thing to everyone. They did not take into account the meaning that many young people attach to doing jail time: that it is not a punishment because inmates get the opportunity to see many of their friends who are already serving time. Recently, the state legislature, led by the governor, has been considering new legislation meant to amend those draconian antidrug laws.

SELLING DRUGS AS A FORM OF WORK

The cultural-normalization model can be linked with the political economy to present a more comprehensive understanding of the drug phenomenon in minority communities throughout the United States. For example, abhorrent as the dominant middle class may find participation in the underground economy of illegal drugs, studies show that illegal drug sales in the inner cities need to be acknowledged as an alternative form of employment (Hamid 1998; Maher 1997; Williams 1989). When you shift the study of illegal drug use from a deviant behavior or social pathology perspective to that of political economy, street drug sales as a form of work cannot be denied. A member of the Fayerville Mayor's Task Force on Drugs, Blight and Violence, Donald McHenry, did not mince words: "Among my people drug dealing is a form of employment."

In the economically depressed inner cities, hustling is another form of employment, and selling drugs is a major part of hustling (Valentine 1978). If illegal drug sales are analyzed as a labor market, the sale of drugs may seem a rational choice for people whose perception is that other forms of work are inaccessible. For example, drug sales pay better and offer Black youths opportunities for apprenticeship in other enterprises in which they can become independent as well as get respect in their own communities.

Not surprisingly, teenagers and young adults who sell drugs in Southland think of their activity as another form of work, just like the young men and women in *Cocaine Kids* (Williams 1989). Some have all the trappings and gadgets that go with what they consider a "cool" businessman. Besides the gold chains and other jewelry, they have adopted symbols of the legitimate business community, such as business cards and cellular phones. The perception of drug dealing as constituting legitimate work is not new; it dates back to the 1960s, as when a young heroin dealer told Prebble and Casey (1969:21): "When I'm on the way home with the bag in my pocket, and I haven't been caught stealing all day, and I didn't get beat up and the cops didn't get me—I feel like a working man coming home [who] worked hard . . . ." It seems that not much has changed in the attitudes of drug dealers.

Most young people who sold drugs on the streets of Fayerville were otherwise unemployed. Only the food industry—local supermarkets and fast-food chains such as McDonald's and Kentucky Fried Chicken (KFC)—offered youths employment opportunities on a regular basis.[1] These fast-food restaurants employed mainly girls; the few young men who worked there were mostly from middle-class homes. The youths most likely to become involved with drugs, males from working-class households, were rarely found working in these establishments. Two of my informants, Gerald and Dread, showed no interest whatsoever in working in fast-food restaurants. They were not only turned off by the low wages, but more important, they felt this kind of work was beneath them. Yet both were high school dropouts with no diplomas! When I suggested that Dread seek employment at the local KFC, he responded, "You must be joking. . . . That's for kids, man."

Like Dread and Gerald most of the young people in Southland did want to work, but not under the conditions commonly set by the employers. While low (often minimum) wages were certainly a part of the problem, they were not the only reason why young people in the Southland shunned regular employment. Some unemployed people in this neighborhood would rather collect empty bottles in the street to claim the five-cent refund per bottle than go to work in a KFC or McDonald's.

While many young people made little money selling drugs, they preferred it to working for somebody else because, it offered them the opportunity to be their own bosses and to earn some respect. It meant that they could choose the hours they worked, which was also important to them since many of them liked to stay out late at night, making a regular nine-to-five job extremely unattractive. As a young homeless man put it to me, "I don't have to answer to nobody telling me what to do." Constant supervision of their work by a White boss was something that most young Black men like Gerald complained about. The young women, on the other hand, tended to complain most about the low wages they received.

Many young people feel an obligation to contribute money to their household. For example, Gerald told me that after his father moved out of the family residence he felt that he had to step in as "the man of the house" to take care of his mother, older sister, and niece. Thus he became more heavily dependent on income from selling illegal drugs. In addition, many youths felt that contributing to the domestic income (even in two-parent households) would earn them the freedom and independence that adult members enjoyed. This felt need for independence, even among teenagers, is related to the importance of individualism as a value in American culture (Spindler and Spindler 1985).

THE CONCEPT OF RESISTANCE

Do minorities sell and use drugs to demonstrate resistance to those in power? The concept of resistance has generated much anthropological interest in the past twenty years. This interest appears in studies of drug use and sales in minority communities, particularly those within the political economy framework. This development has produced many solid works and is likely to continue well into the twenty-first century (see, e.g., Maher 1997; Waterston 1993).

Although the political economy framework and an emphasis on resistance are important to comprehensive understanding of the drug phenomenon, the concept of resistance can be misleading. As anthropologist Stephen Schensul (1997:57–69) correctly points out, whether involvement with illegal drugs is a form of resistance or protest in class warfare is an empirical question whose answer must be demonstrated, not assumed. To assume drug use or peddling drugs is a form of resistance presupposes an awareness of oppression and organized resistance symbolized by drug use where it may actually not be occurring.

In Southland there is a general awareness of the oppression of Black people, but I would argue that it is superficial, and resistance, if there is any, can hardly be described as organized. People may or may not be reacting against (or resisting) the oppressive impact of larger structures. For example, if a person sees him/herself as "working" by selling drugs, is he or she resisting the capitalist economy or enjoying its benefits? The entrepreneurial spirit that many of my informants express as their goal indicates that they want to be part of the capitalist system. They feel politically powerless, that is, not represented in the political arena, and accept what seems to be the widespread American pattern: that those with money will be heard and can make an impact on society. To this extent, these people believe that working within the capitalist system rather than resisting it will help them achieve social mobility as well as political power. Most of these young people, including Gerald and Dread, maintain that they sell drugs in anticipation of raising capital and seed money to begin working toward their realization of the American Dream.

DIFFERENCES IN PERCEPTION

My ethnographic findings do not conjure up images of a drug addict as a despised individual whose morals are debased or a person necessarily predisposed to antisocial behavior, criminal behavior, or both. The person whose lifestyle most resembled that of the middle-class perception of a drug addict was that of the crackhead in the late 1980s and early 1990s. But as time went by, people learned more about the experience of crack smoking and have managed to control its undesirable physical as well as psychological effects, so that even the crackhead is no longer automatically considered a "pariah" in this community. This change is similar to that reported as having occurred in the 1960s and 1970s with regard to pot smokers and LSD poppers (Becker 1986a:47–66).

In Southland, a "drug user" is not perceived as an out-of-control drug addict or a criminal or swindler. People who use drugs are not necessarily drug addicts who cannot function in society or perform their daily chores at a regular pace. Most people who use and/or sell drugs in Southland did not fit the stereotypical image of the junkie or drug addict who is disabled by the intoxicating effect of the drug he/she consumes. Marijuana, the most common drug of choice (i.e., the drug used by the largest number of residents in this community), was smoked in moderation. Even though the phrase "getting high" was used to describe a person under the influence of marijuana, rarely did this person behave in a socially unacceptable manner or in a way different from how he/she behaved prior to smoking the marijuana joint. In addition, persons showing visible signs of deterioration were not shunned because of their drug use per se, but rather because of antisocial behavior such as not keeping oneself clean or being known to steal to support their drug use.

I came across so few addicts in the classic sense of the term in this community that I am surprised at the use of this label. Young people in particular rejected such labels as addicts, junkies, potheads, and crackheads, except when they were used to taunt or show disrespect to others. On the other hand, their parents may have used these terms to warn them about the consequences of drug use. This is exactly what happened to Gerald. His father called him a crackhead partly to shame him in the hope that he would give up smoking crack. Gerald was furious at this label because it implied that he had lost control of his drug use and was thought to exhibit behavior that was seen as negative by others. Gerald felt he was not a crackhead and that his father's remarks were an insult as well as a provocation—a challenge that he couldn't back off or walk away from.

MISCONCEPTIONS

At the time of my fieldwork, the local news media attributed widespread illegal drug activities in Southland to youth gangs, although little evidence existed to support such a claim. The police certainly knew that gangs did not control drug distribution in this neighborhood; it was mostly in the hands of independent entrepreneurs because the leaders of the organized distribution rings had all been caught and were serving long sentences. There were two or three close-knit youth crews or posses, but they were linked to other crimes such as automobile theft, assault, vandalism of public property, and possession of weapons. Fayerville eliminated its organized crime in the 1970s and '80s, and the youth gangs' level of involvement with the drug trade was nowhere near that of gangs in places such as New York City, Chicago, Los Angeles, or Kansas City.

Sensationalist media reports of Black youths' violent behavior as induced by taking drugs and exemplified by turf battles among rival drug gangs obscure understanding the drug phenomenon. At the same time they also add a layer of complexity to understanding community behavior in regard to illegal drug use and sales. Not only are the media stereotypes inaccurate, but they perpetuate animosities and hostilities between ethnic groups, contribute to polarization between Blacks and Whites, and lead to such abuses as racial profiling. Ethnographically based research can help significantly to undermine these stereotypes.

Another factor that contributes to misconceptions of the so-called drug problem in the inner cities is the need on the part of state and municipal authorities, including law enforcement agencies, to get federal funds for their local programs. In 1990, the city of Fayerville failed to qualify for a federal grant to fight illegal drugs because the funds were targeted to municipalities in which youth gangs were known to distribute drugs. This prompted officials of the city of Fayerville to reclassify the three Jamaican crews or posses as "gangs" with organized crime structures and emphasize their role in the drug trade, in the hope that Southland might qualify for such funding in the future. Ethnographic research can provide relevant data—an accurate and complete account of inner-city behavior—useful in formulating more flexible and thus more effective drug policies, pointing to the need for not one type but for different types of drug policies.

GENDER AND DRUGS

When studying drug use among women, the temptation of the psychological approach to emphasize women's psychological dependency and victimization is so overwhelming that many of us fail to see that women are not necessarily victims. Lisa Maher effectively critiques this assumption in her study of women's involvement in the drug trade in Brooklyn. In describing and presenting the personal narratives of these women, Maher writes:

> I have tried to create a space between the twin discourses of victimization and volition (agency) that inform current understandings of women's drug-related lawbreaking. While this space must be large enough to include the constraints of sexism, racism, and poverty that structure the lives of these women, it cannot be so big as to overwhelm the active, creative, and often contradictory choices, adaptations, and resistances that constitute women's criminal agencies. (1997:201)

Maher's quote applies perfectly to my study of Black youths.

This viewpoint allows for the individuality of the lives presented here as well as for all the individuality that resides in all communities. For example, while race, as it intersects with class and to some extent gender, is a constraint on occupational choices for many Black youths, within that constraint individuals make different choices and combine resistance to and participation in the larger structures of society in different ways. Liz, for example, the only young person not using or selling drugs, sought a way out of the constraints of race, religion, and gender by choosing to go to college, which afforded her an opportunity to expand her world and therefore be less bound by her constraints. At the same time Denise, the daughter of a Jamaican immigrant who is a mid-level executive of a major high-tech corporation, chose to evade constraints at home by joining the "womanish girls," who were independent "street girls" (not streetwalkers or prostitutes). Similarly, race and gender interact differently for males: some, like many of the respondents in Katherine Newman's (1999) study of inner-city youths who work in the fast-food industry, are willing to take minimum-wage, low-skilled, and dead-end jobs as a way up and out, while others, for example Gerald, choose the entrepreneurial role of drug sales.

CONCLUSION

The models social scientists create must reflect empirical reality; otherwise they distort the social phenomena we have declared to be studying (Becker 1986b). The danger is that such distortions could easily become the basis for policies that fail to rectify "social problems," as has happened so far with the war on drugs.[2] The cultural-normalization model that I use is based on my position that an explanatory model must reflect not just the empirical realities of the local community, but also the reality of the relationship between the local community and the national political economy of which it is an integral part. Critical medical anthropologists (Singer, et al. 1992) share this viewpoint. No local community is an island unto itself. Every local community is linked to regional and national political economies. Consequently, we should avoid "a myopia that sharply delineates the behavior at close range but obscures the less proximate and less visible structures and processes that engender and sustain that behavior" (di Leonardo 1998:121).

As Micaela di Leonardo (1998) correctly points out, too frequently anthropologists, through their micro-level ethnographic studies, inadvertently reinforce the stereotypes about the underclass with all its moral perjorativeness and perpetuate the view that there are no connections between "them" and "us." The goal of productive, critical anthropology must be to link the levels of sociocultural institutions so that the connections between the micro and macro levels become clear. The gaps between these levels can be filled by ethnographies that incorporate description and analysis of middle-level institutions, which, in this case, include not only the peer group but also the school, the community center, the church, and most important, the extended family.

NOTES

[1] See Katherine Newman (1998), *No Shame In My Game,* about the situation in Harlem, New York.

[2] See, e.g., Ethan Nadelmann's (1998) critique of this so-called war on drugs and his passionate plea for trying an alternative method such as harm reduction.

References

Agar, Michael. 1996. *The professional stranger: An informal introduction to ethnography*. New York: Academic Press.

Anderson, Elijah. 1980. Some observations on Black youth employment. In Bernard Anderson and Isabel Sawhill (eds.), *Youth employment and public policy*. Englewood Cliffs, NJ: Prentice Hall.

Anderson, Elijah. 1990. *Streetwise: Race, class, and change in an urban community*. Chicago: The University of Chicago Press.

Babbie, Earl R. 1998. *Survey research methods*. Belmont, CA: Wadsworth.

Becker, Howard S., ed. 1964. *Perspectives on deviance: The other side*. New York: The Free Press.

Becker, Howard S. 1986a. *Doing things together: Selected papers*. Evanston, IL: Northwestern University Press.

Becker, Howard S. 1986b. *Writing for social scientists*. Chicago: The University of Chicago Press.

Bourgois, Philippe. 1995. *In search of respect: Selling crack in El Barrio*. New York: Cambridge Press.

Brown, Claude. 1965. *Manchild in the promised land*. New York: New American Library, Inc.

Carpenter, Cheryl et al. 1988. *Kids, drugs, and crime*. Lexington, MA: D. C. Heath and Company.

Comitas, L. 1983. Occupational multiplicity in rural Jamaica. In *Work and family life: West Indian perspectives*. New York: Anchor Press.

Dei, Kojo A. 1996. *Illicit drugs and minority youths in a low-income urban neighborhood*. Columbia University/Ann Arbor, MI: UMI.

di Leonardo, Micaela. 1998. *Exotics at home: Anthropologies, others, American modernity*. Chicago: The University of Chicago Press.

Donaldson, Greg. 1993. *The ville: Cops and kids in urban America*. New York: Anchor Books.

Dreher, Melanie. 1982. *Working men and ganja: Marihuana use in rural Jamaica*. Philadelphia: Institute for the Study of Human Issues.

Geertz, Clifford. 1973. *The interpretation of cultures*. New York: Basic Books.

Gibbs, Jewelle Taylor, ed. 1988. *Young, black, and male in America: An endangered species*. Dover, MA: Auburn House Publishing Company.

Glassner, Barry, and Julia Loughlin. 1987. *Drugs in adolescent worlds*. New York: St. Martin's Press.

Goode, Erich. 1999. *Drugs in American society*. 5th Edition. New York: McGraw-Hill.

Gwaltney, John L. 1981. Common sense and science: Urban core Black observations. In *Anthropologists at home in North America*. New York: Cambridge University Press.

Gwaltney, John L. 1993. *Drylongso: A self-portrait of Black America*. New York: New Press [1980].

Hamid, Ansley. 1992. Drugs and patterns of opportunity in the inner city: The case of middle-aged, middle-income cocaine smokers. In Adele V. Harrell and George E. Peterson (eds.), *Drugs, crime, and social isolation*. Washington, DC: Urban Institute

Hamid, Ansley. 1998. *Drugs in America: Sociology, economics, and politics*. Gaithersburg, MD: Aspen Publishers, Inc.

Hannerz, Ulf. 1969. *Soulside: Inquiries into ghetto culture and community*. New York: Columbia University Press.

Harrell, Adele V., and George E. Peterson. 1992. *Drugs, crime, and social isolation: Barriers to urban opportunity*. Washington, DC: The Urban Institute Press.

Johnson, Bruce D. 1980. Toward a theory of drug subcultures. In Dan Littieri et al. (eds.), *Theories on Drug Abuse*. Rockville, MD: NIDA

Jones, Delmos J. 1995. Anthropology and the oppressed: A reflection on "native" anthropology. In E. L. Cerroni-Long (ed.), *Insider Anthropology*. NAPA Bulletin, 16.

Keesing, Roger M. 2000. Nor a real fish: The ethnographer as inside outsider. In Philip R. DeVita (ed.), *Stumbling toward truth: Anthropologists at work*. Prospect Heights, IL: Waveland Press.

Knipe, Ed. 1995. *Culture, society, and drugs: The social science approach to drug use*. Prospect Heights, IL: Waveland Press.

Liebow, Elliot. 1967. *Tally's corner*. Boston: Little, Brown & Company.

Lusane, Clarence. 1991. *Pipe dream blues: Racism and the war on drugs*. Boston: South End Press.

Maher, Lisa. 1997. *Sexed work: Gender, race and resistance in a Brooklyn drug market*. New York: Oxford University Press.

Martin, Elmer P., and Joanne Mitchell Martin. 1978. *The Black extended family*. Chicago: The University of Chicago Press.

Mead, Margaret. 1970. *Culture and commitment: A study of the generation gap*. New York: Natural History Press/Doubleday & Co.

Merton, Robert K., and Elinor Barber. 1963. Sociological ambivalence. In E. Tiryakian (ed.), *Sociological theory: Values and sociocultural change*. New York: Free Press.

Musto, David. 1973. *The American disease: Origins of narcotic control*. New Haven, CT: Yale University Press.

Nadelmann, Ethan. 1998, January–February. Experimenting with drugs. *Foreign Affairs*, 111–126.

National Institute on Drug Abuse (NIDA). 1991. *National household survey on drug abuse*. Rockville, MD: DHHS Publication.

Newman, Katherine S. 1999. *No shame in my game: The working poor in the inner city*. New York: Alfred A. Knopf and The Russell Sage Foundation.

Nobles, Wade W. 1984. Alienation, human transformation and adolescent drug use: Toward a reconceptualization of the problem. *Journal of Drug Issues* 1: 243–252.

Ogbu, John. 1978. *Minority education and caste*. New York: Academic Press.

Ogbu, John. 1991. Immigrant and involuntary minorities in comparative perspective. In *Minority status and schooling*. New York: Garland.

Partridge, William L. 1985. *The hippie ghetto: The natural history of a subculture*. Prospect Heights, IL: Waveland Press.

Prebble, E., and J. Casey. 1969. Taking care of business: The heroin user's life on the streets. *International Journal of the Addiction* 4:1–24.

Ratner, Mitchell S. ed. 1993. *Crack pipe as pimp: An ethnographic investigation of sex-for-crack exchanges*. New York: Lexington Books.

Ray, Oakley, and Charles Ksir. 1996. *Drugs, society, and human behavior*. Seventh Edition. New York: Mosby.

Rubin, Vera, and Lambros Comitas. 1975. *Ganja in Jamaica*. The Hague: Mouton.

Schensul, Stephen L. 1997. Anthropologists & medicine. *Critical Reviews in Anthropology* 26(1): 57–69.

Sharff, Jagna W. 1998. *King Kong on 4th Street: Families and the violence of poverty on the Lower East Side*. Boulder, CO: Westview Press.

Singer, Merrill, Freddie Valentin, Hans Baer, and Zhongke Jia. 1992. Why does Juan Garcia have a drinking problem? The perspective of critical medical anthropology. *Medical Anthropology* 14:77–108.

Spindler, George, and Louise Spindler. 1985. Foreword. In William L. Partridge (ed.), *The hippie ghetto: The natural history of a subculture*. Prospect Heights, IL: Waveland Press.

Urban League. 1998. *Annual Report: The State of Black America*.

Valentine, Bettylou. 1978. *Hustling and other hard work: Life styles in the ghetto*. New York: The Free Press.

Washington Post. 28 July 1995.

Waterston, Alice. 1993. *Street addicts in the political economy*. Philadelphia: Temple University Press.

West, Cornell. 1993. *Race matters*. Boston: Beacon Press.

Williams, Terry. 1989. *Cocaine kids*. Reading, MA: Addison-Wesley.

Williams, Terry M., and William Kornblum. 1985. *Growing up poor*. Lexington, MA: D.C. Heath and Company.

Wilson, William Julius. 1987. *The truly disadvantaged: The inner city, the underclass, and public policy*. Chicago: The University of Chicago Press.

Winick, Charles. 1986. The deviance model of drug taking behavior: A critique. *Drugs and Society* 1(1): 29–49.

Study Guide

Prepared by
Irene Glasser
Center for Alcohol and Addiction Studies
Brown University

In writing the study guide to Kojo Dei's fine ethnography, I have tried to provide some of the historical and anthropological contexts of the work. I have focused on the crucial points that I would personally underline in teaching this book. I have also suggested some student assignments (some short-term and some semester-long) that would supplement *Ties That Bind* and would encourage the student's own creativity in the anthropological endeavor.

CHAPTER 1

Like other urban ethnographers before him, Dei spent a long time (over ten years) entering the cultures of one urban neighborhood in order to discover the social context of involvement in illegal drugs among the youth of a predominantly Black neighborhood, Southland, one section of Fayerville, a suburb of a major city in the Northeast United States.

Underlying much of Dei's work is a search for the *emic* or "native" point of view of the community under study. The term emic is derived from *phomenic* from the field of linguistic anthropology. It refers to the minimal unit of sound that is recognized by a native speaker. The emic point of view then is the native point of view. This is a contrast to the *etic* (derived from the term *phonetic*) which refers to categories derived by outsiders and then applied to a culture (see Lavender and Schultz, *Core Concepts in Cultural Anthropology*, for a discussion of emic and etic).

The search for the emic point of view led Dei to discover quickly that, despite the concern of politicians both inside and outside Southland, newspaper articles, and official statements, drug dealing was *not* considered a major problem by the local residents. Rather, overcrowded housing, income, employment, financial assistance (welfare), family dynamics, and the lack of recreational activities were the true concerns of the community. Further, alcohol and tobacco use, not drugs, were thought to be the major public health risks of the community. How do you think this disparity between Southland community concerns and the larger society came to be?

The title of chapter 1 is "Minorities and Drugs." Discuss the limits of the word "minority." Does this refer to a numerical minority within all of the United States, or is it a reference to a lack of power? Is "minority" a reference to the endemic racism toward people of color, deriving from the era of slavery? Does the term imply a monolithic cultural category, which Dei tells us does *not* exist? Does the use of the term actually encourage us to ignore the important cultural differences between, for example, the African-American community and the Jamaican community? Finally, does the term "minority" only focus on ethnic or racial categories, ignoring social class?

In your own communities, what is meant when people say "minority"? What would be more specific and accurate in describing the ethnic and cultural groups you know? How does social class intersect with ethnicity and race in your communities?

CHAPTER 2

As an anthropologist who comes from a village in Ghana, how is Dei positioned to conduct his ethnography? How does Dei's experience of the roles of elders and sense of community identity differ from that of his key informants? What were the advantages Dei had in being a Black man from Africa? What were any sources of resentment or distrust regarding his outsider/insider status?

Often the best research is propelled by a question that cannot be easily answered. In *Ties That Bind* Dei is trying to understand the paradox between "on the one hand, the reported concerns and hostility of community residents toward illegal drugs and on the other hand, the heavy participation of local youths' involvement in using and selling these same drugs" (pp. 32–33). This paradox is even more compelling, considering that Dei found out early in his study that drug use and trade had been pushed indoors, and so was being done within the confines of the family.

Dei uses the technique of *triangulation of data* in order to understand the place of drugs in Southland. This means that he utilized several research strategies at the same time, and analyzed the results, always being sensitive for not only consistencies, but also for contradictions in the data.

For each research technique, list the advantages and limitations of the strategy for uncovering the truth. Also, discuss how these methods can work together to gain a full understanding of the cultural context of drugs. (For further reading in the use of anthropological research strategies see H. Russell Bernard's *Handbook of Methods in Cultural Anthropology*.)

Qualitative Methods
  Life histories (with five Southland youth)
  Ethnographic interviews
  Participant observation
  Folk seminars/focus groups
  Archival research (newspaper articles over a period of time)

Quantitative Methods
  Household surveys (24 completed surveys)
  Youth surveys (50 respondents)

A major theme related to drugs in Southland is *ambivalence*. On the one hand, the drug trade is a source of money and independence. On the other hand, it leads to violence, sickness, and potential time spent in jail. How are these ambivalent attitudes expressed, especially by the adults of the community?

Occasionally, Dei is told to "mind your own business." What are the reasons for this hostility? What are the sources of reciprocity that Dei employed that enabled him to "give back" to the community and overcome such hostility. How does understanding the reasons for the reluctance of some members of the Southland community itself become data for this study?

In the early days of anthropology the communities under study were far from the anthropologist's home (consider a classic such as *Coming of Age in Samoa* by Margaret Mead). Further, the resulting books and papers were usually written in the language of the anthropologist, not of the communities under study. As anthropology moved "home" and urban anthropology in North American, Latin America, and Europe became more common, we often hear objections to our very presence (though these objections may not be discussed in print). In my own ethnography of a soup kitchen in the United States (see *More Than Bread: Ethnography of a Soup Kitchen*), I quickly discovered that although people were friendly and willing to talk to me within the confines of the soup kitchen dining room, once back out on the street, many of the people whom I recognized would not make eye contact with me. I eventually understood this as their disappointment that their life had led them to spending their daytime hours in a soup kitchen, and also their not wanting to answer the question that might be posed by their acquaintances, "how do you know her?" My strategy for respecting the privacy of the people I met in the soup kitchen became *not* to make eye contact on the street with the soup kitchen guest until he or she acknowledged me.

Dei's ethnography brings to mind other excellent urban ethnographies including James Spradley's *You Owe Yourself A Drunk*, Carol Stack's *All Our Kin: Strategies for Survival in a Black Community*, George Gmelch's *The Irish Tinkers: The Urbanization of an Itinerant People*, Philippe Bourgois's *In Search of Respect: Selling Crack in El Barrio*, and Joseph Howell's *Hard Living on Clay Street: Portraits of Blue Collar Families*. Choosing one or more of these ethnographies, compare and contrast the methodologies and major findings with *Ties That Bind*.

Dei's use of life histories also brings to mind other life histories. For an in-depth assignment, compare and contrast Dei's five life histories with Marjorie Shostak's *Nisa*, Ruth Behar's *Translated Woman*, and Sharon Gmelch's *Nan*. How do the details of one person's life "fill out" the subtleties and inherent contradictions within members of a culture?

CHAPTER 3

Gerald was a 16-year-old who was heavily involved in the drug trade, selling marijuana, cocaine, crack, heroin, and angel dust on a regular basis. He had already dropped out of school, and was a regular user of marijuana. Despite this picture, Gerald was still well liked in the neighborhood, was seen as coming from a good family, contributed to his family's income, and still had dreams of becoming a great musician and successful in the music industry as a producer. In other words, Dei shows us, through Gerald's story, not the stereotypical picture of a young man from a "dysfunctional" family, who had been raised by a single mother on welfare, but a young man from an intact family where both parents are employed. How can you explain the differences between the dominant society's judgment of Gerald's and that of his own community?

How is Dei able to be close to this family, who perhaps would not usually be open to an outsider knowing their intimate concerns? Is Dei himself becoming an elder (in terms of status and wisdom) for the family? How does this affect the research?

Throughout this chapter, Dei uses direct quotes from Gerald, his father, mother, sister, the neighborhood storyteller, and Gerald's maternal uncle. When do you believe it is best to use the words of one's key informants? Are there certain words in this chapter (e.g., buddha, softie) that are a special key for understanding the worldview of the culture Dei is presenting?

Gerald's first experience with drugs was economic, when, as a 12-year-old, he was a lookout for older boys on his block who sold drugs (p. 64). Most of Gerald's motivations to be involved in drugs appeared to be economic. How does this contrast with the dominant psychological explanation for adolescent drug use?

Among the meta-themes of this chapter are a sense of fatalism, loyalty within a family (especially between mother and son), a feeling of independence, and the quest for respect. Discuss cultures with which you are familiar in which any or all of these are also highly valued.

CHAPTER 4

Akosua, like other people of Southland, appeared to reserve the term "drug addiction" for those who used heroin (p. 78). Why do you think this occurred, and does this insight have public health policy implications for campaigns to deter adolescent drug use?

Make a chart of the most dangerous to the least dangerous drugs based on the emic point of view in Southland as expressed by Akosua.

One of the reasons that Akosua says that she sold drugs was that she was dependent on the social welfare department who controlled her life in exchange for modest amounts of financial assistance (p. 93). Do you think that a more generous welfare system would be a deterrent to involvement in the drug trade? Is there in fact less of a drug trade in countries with a more generous welfare system?

CHAPTER 5

Dread was a 22-year-old "baccra massa" (entrepreneur) who was born and raised in Jamaica and came to the United States to join his mother Colleen when he was 19 years old. His story, and especially his relationship with his extended family, illustrates the ambivalent attitudes toward drugs. On the one hand, many of the men of Dread's family smoked marijuana, but did place limits on its use (for example, Mr. Morris's discrete use of marijuana, p. 103). Dread's mother, although continually frustrated by his unwillingness to go to school or work, and very frightened of the strong probability that he too would end up in jail like his older brother, appreciated the use of Dread's car (bought through drug sales) in order to keep her job cleaning offices in the middle of the night. There was also the belief in the medicinal use of marijuana as a cure for many ailments (p. 97). Discuss the cultural significance of marijuana within the Jamaican community. Is there any way in which to reconcile this emic view of marijuana with the present U.S. drug policy?

We see in this chapter good examples of police attitudes toward youths in the Jamaican community and youths in the African-American community (p. 98). This favoring of one ethnic group over another by the dominant society has examples in other places in the world. It is sometimes seen as a "divide and conquer" strategy that inhibits alliances between less powerful groups from forming. Do you know of other examples of this throughout the world?

In immersing himself in the life of the community, Dei was able to observe directly Dread's selling of crack, although this is something that Dread had always verbally denied (p. 101). Anthropologists' ability to observe *behavior* directly in contrast to relying on what is told during an interview is one of the distinguishing features of anthropology. For example, anthropologist Paul Koegel, in exploring the survival strategies of the homeless mentally ill, found a man living on the street who claimed to get no help from any agency. However, one Sunday morning, in making his rounds, Koegel observed him as he received his weekly cooler of food distributed by an organization (Koegel 1992).

In the period of the study, Dread had episodes of drug dealing, not working, and working in legal occupations (fixing things and cutting hair). Dei challenges the pervasive labeling that often occurs by outsiders, who would call Dread a "drug dealer." In my own work with the homeless, I too have found that the label "the homeless" limits our understanding when applied to people who, in reality, often cycle between living in apartments, with friends and relatives, in shelters, and, at times, on the streets (Glasser and Bridgman 1999).

In the following excerpt, we see Dei as a respected elder in his field setting, as Colleen poses the following question after her husband Geoffrey leaves the household because his stepsons won't behave as he wants them to:

"No man abandons his family because the children are hard headed. Tell me, Mr. Kojo, if what he is saying makes sense?" (p. 110).

What do you believe is the proper response of the anthropologist when key informants try to engage him or her in their lives?

CHAPTER 6

Denise came to the United States from Jamaica as a seven-year-old girl, joining her extended family in Southland. After trying to get along in her father's house (which included her stepmother, Rosemary), Denise joined her grandmother's household. The extended family is often viewed as a strength of families from traditional cultures, but how able is Grandma Osetta to supervise 15-year-old Denise on the streets of a new culture (refer to p. 119)? Have we romanticized the extended family as being able to provide the guidance and supervision that a child's own parents might provide?

Like many U. S. teens, Denise is especially sensitive to hypocrisy and inconsistency from her elders, who tell her to behave one way (don't use drugs), but show a tolerance at other times for drug use. What are some of the inconsistencies evidenced by both Denise's stepmother, Rosemary, and Grandma Osetta in their attitudes toward drugs?

What do you see as Denise's future, now that she has spent some time in jail and has a baby, who is being cared for primarily by Grandma Osetta and Aunt Cherry? What would you suggest for this young woman, who was once so full of promise?

CHAPTER 7

The reality of conducting research is that one usually needs a proposal that includes a detailed research plan. Yet, in the case of including Liz's story in Dei's ethnographic research, it was Liz and her mother, Mrs. Payne, who were the clear advocates for this. Believing in "learning from the community" and being flexible, Dei agreed. Discuss how different *Ties That Bind* would have been without Liz's story. How can the research proposal itself accommodate important changes in strategy that can only occur *after* immersion in the field?

Why is Liz so resilient to the potential influences of her neighbors and peers? Why has she not become involved with drugs, dropped out of school, and become a teenage mother? In addition to the love of her mother and father, their openness in their communication style with her, and the family involvement in a church, was the fact that her parents did not forbid Liz to talk with other members of the neighborhood. Liz was not perceived as a "snob" by her friends of Southland, and she was encouraged to be herself and stand firm in her convictions. Liz also was able to observe that her girlfriends who had babies as teenagers were in reality rarely raising the children themselves.

Is there anything in Liz's story that could be taught to other youths in Southland? A long-term research project could be to find exemplary community development projects within communities like Southland, that have been successful in promoting adolescents on the road to success.

CHAPTER 8

Now that we have come to the concluding chapter of *Ties That Bind*, review the cultural-normalization model (pp. 30–31) that guided Dei throughout his work. How successful was Dei in being "actor-oriented" so that the interpretation of culture was constructed by the community members? Was there anything missing from Dei's *thick* description of culture, which was Clifford Geertz's term for the writing that emerges in the search for insider meanings? How different would Dei's work have been had he been guided by the deviant behavior, drug subculture, or political economy theories?

Dei urges us to reconsider the draconian drug laws that have put so many young people in jail and prison for drug use and drug sales. If jail is *not* a deterrent for many members of Southland, is this the wisest policy? Since so many people told Dei that they saw drug dealing as a form of employment, shouldn't that be a major focus of anti-drug programs?

One explanation for drug dealing is that it is a form of resistance to those in power. However, Dei came to see a person's immersion in the drug trade as an expression of his or her embracing of capitalism and wanting very much to be successful in "the system." Dei suggests here that imputing an organized resistance as the driving force of the drug trade may be an example of superimposing a theory onto a culture without adequate evidence to support the theory. What have you learned about the concept of resistance from Dei's key informants?

Finally, Dei came to Southland expecting to see "drug addicts" as they are so often depicted by the media (thin, hungry, dirty, and violent). But the majority of drug using youths in this study did not conform to this image. Do you think that there is a media stereotype, or do you think that the Southland is not representative of communities in the rest of the United States?

Kojo Dei is a voice for residents of communities like Southland. What do you imagine the reaction of Southland's residents might be as they read *Ties That Bind*?

REFERENCES

Behar, Ruth. 1993. *Translated woman: Crossing the border with Esperanza's story*. Boston: Beacon Press.

Bernard, H. Russell. 1998. *Handbook of methods in cultural anthropology*. Walnut Creek, CA: AltaMira Press.

Bourgois, Philippe. 1995. *In search of respect: Selling crack in El Barrio*. New York: Cambridge Press.

Glasser, Irene. 1988. *More than bread: Ethnography of a soup kitchen*. Tuscaloosa: University of Alabama Press.

Glasser, Irene and Rae Bridgman. 1999. *Braving the street: The anthropology of homelessness*. New York: Berghahn Books.

Gmelch, George. 1985. *Irish Tinkers: The urbanization of an itinerant people*, 2nd ed. Prospect Heights, IL: Waveland Press.

Gmelch, Sharon. 1986. *Nan: The life of an Irish travelling woman*. Prospect Heights, IL: Waveland Press.

Howell, Joseph T. 1973. *Hard living on clay street: Portraits of blue collar families*. Prospect Heights, IL: Waveland Press.

Koegel, Paul. 1992. "Through a different lens: An anthropological perspective on the homeless mentally ill." *Culture, Medicine, and Psychiatry* 16(1): 1–22.

Lavender, Robert H. and Emily A. Schultz. 2000. *Core concepts in cultural anthropology*. Mountain View, CA: Mayfield.

Mead, Margaret. 1928. *Coming of age in Samoa: A psychological study of primitive youth for western civilization*. New York: William Morrow.

Shostak, Marjorie. 1981. *Nisa, the life and words of a !Kung woman*. Cambridge, MA: Harvard University Press.

Spradley, James. 1970. *You owe yourself a drunk: An ethnography of urban nomads*. Boston: Little, Brown. Reissued Prospect Heights, IL: Waveland Press, 2000.

Stack, Carol. 1974. *All our kin: Strategies for survival in a Black community*. New York: Harper & Row.